The Pennine Way

£1.50

Other Dalesman books on long-distance walks:

THE CLEVELAND WAY
THE CROSSES WALK
THE CUMBRIA WAY
THE DALES WAY
THE DERWENT WAY
THE EBOR WAY
LYKE WAKE WALK
THE PEAKLAND WAY
WHITE ROSE WALK
THE WOLDS WAY

The Pennine Way

Britain's Longest Continuous Footpath

by
Kenneth Oldham

Dalesman Books
1979

The Dalesman Publishing Company Ltd.
Clapham (via Lancaster), North Yorkshire

© Kenneth Oldham 1960, 1979

First published 1960
Eighth edition 1979

ISBN: 0 85206 508 6

TO TOM STEPHENSON

No other name is so connected
with the Way

Printed by Galava Printing Co. Ltd.
Hallam Road, Nelson, Lancashire

Contents

The maps on pages 10, 21, 33, 41, 56 and 63 are drawn by
E. Jeffrey.

Cover photograph of Penyghent from near Horton by
W.R. Mitchell.

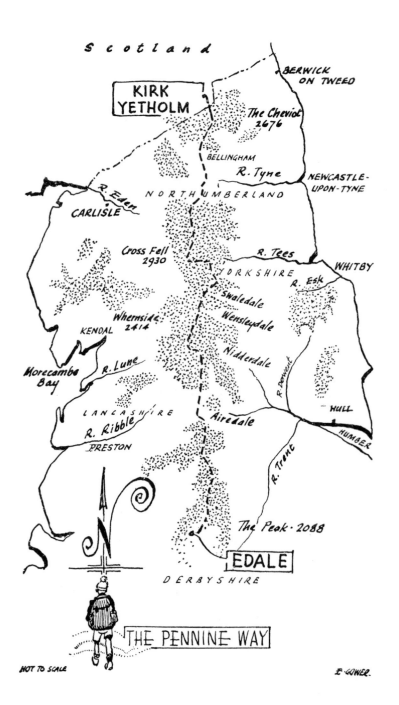

Scotland

BERWICK ON TWEED

KIRK YETHOLM

The Cheviot 2676

BELLINGHAM

R. Tyne

NEWCASTLE-UPON-TYNE

NORTHUMBERLAND

R. Eden

CARLISLE

Cross Fell 2930

R. Tees

YORKSHIRE

R. Esk

WHITBY

Swaledale

Wensleydale

Whernside 2414

KENDAL

Nidderdale

R. Derwent

Morecambe Bay

R. Lune

LANCASHIRE

R. Ribble

Airedale

HULL

HUMBER

PRESTON

R. Trent

N

The Peak · 2088

EDALE

DERBYSHIRE

THE PENNINE WAY

NOT TO SCALE

E. GOWER.

Introducing the Pennine Way

I'd have him grow
deep-breathed, deep-hearted,
cherished of wind and snow;
loving delightful laughter, and harsh thrills
in summer rivers and on
    perilous hills.
        —Geoffrey Winthrop Young.

On Saturday, 24th April, 1965, the National Parks Commission celebrated the completion of the Pennine Way, Britain's first long distance footpath, at an open air gathering near Malham Tarn, Yorkshire. Amongst the speakers were Mr F.T. Willey, Minister of Land and Natural Resources, and Mr. Tom Stephenson, secretary of the Ramblers' Association, who first thought of the idea of the Pennine Way—a two hundred and fifty mile footpath route linking Derbyshire to Scotland—some thirty years before. Movements are afoot to connect other footpath lengths to its northern limits but the present route has the peculiar fascination of a good book. The more you sample, the more certain it is that you will not be satisfied until you have read the final chapter. Unlike reading, however, you can tackle it from either end or sample random sections from the middle. Whatever your choice, you will not fail to be enthused by its challenge, the more rewarding in that interwoven with the physical endeavour, is a wealth of interest in many varied fields. Whether you are a naturalist, historian or geologist, or simply enjoy hill walking, the Pennine Way will more than satisfy your needs.

From the sudden plunge from the bright greens of Edale's pastures into the deep "V" shaped clough of Grindsbrook and the almost lunar landscape of wasting peat and bogs of the Derbyshire summits, the Pennine Way leads through a veritable wilderness for the first arduous thirty five miles. My first introduction was in 1952, when with colleague Harry Stopford and seven boys aged 13 to 14, we traversed the route in 17 days. Out of this came 14 days of rain—not just the odd shower, but a deluge. Everywhere, streams and rivers were in spate, while an incessant tattoo beat upon our capes as we laboured with eternal squelching across mist-shrouded moors—exasperating at times, yet so completely rewarding in the end. Out of trial and tribulation came the splendour of the scene, of a rainbow with the field of gold, and above all else, the fury of the Tees! By contrast, similar parties of boys from Nelson traversed the whole route in 1959 and again in 1967 with only one light shower on either journey; the former group even walking in August — a notorious time for rain in the Pennines. A further group in 1966 crossed Kinder in deep snow (mid-April) and experienced heat wave conditions before they crossed the Cheviots. In 1975 and 1976, others endured continuous heatwave and drought throughout.

The experiences of these and many other parties have provided a wealth of material which forms the basis of this book. No descriptive attempt is made to provide a substitute for the map and compass for the minute details of stiles and gates will change while the basic landscape will remain. The author aims to cover those details of the Pennine Way which the map does not show, and to pass on some of the enjoyment of the trail. The final chapter describes the organisation which underlies the planning of a successful traverse of the Way.

The 16 day plan for the traverse allows time to enjoy the scenic splendours of the Way. Other folk might prefer the physical challenge of a speedy traverse and Dave Scott of Colne told me that the group relay record has now been seized by the Holmfirth Harriers, a hill tribe from the boundaries of the Dark Peak! No doubt their local training grounds proved more than adequate for this tremendous feat of completing the Way in less than thirty hours. The record for the individual crossing is held by Peter Dawes of Ulverston who traversed the route in three days, one hour and forty-eight minutes at the age of thirty-six. John North of Rawtenstall might receive equal acclaim for his incredible cyclo-cross in June 1978, when he achieved the south to north crossing in two days, eight hours and forty-five minutes. As chairman of the Clayton le Moors Harriers, who formerly held the relay record, he prefers straight running, and when asked how he kept going at such an intense pace his reply echoed the mountaineer's golden rule: "Eat a little and often." Those who wish to traverse the Way at whatever speed, take note.

A 16-Day Traverse of the Pennine Way

Day 1: Kinder and Bleaklow —Edale to Crowden

O.S. 1:50 000 Map Series Sheet 110 (Sheffield and Huddersfield), or the new O.S. 1:25 000 Outdoor Leisure Map "The Dark Peak".

Allow 7 hours. 15 miles.   Total 15 miles.

Edale is sheltered by the high summits which stretch from Kinder's blackened edge on the north and which sweep round to the west to join the brown grassy ridge of Rushup Edge and Mam Tor on the south. These southern flanks lie steep with folds and ridges marking landslips of the shale, and from them, the whole panorama of Edale lies before.

Across the valley, the foot of Grindsbrook is clearly marked by a woodland cleft, and it is here, beyond the church and the *Nag's Head Inn* that our journey will commence. A fallen tree-trunk spanning Grindsbrook at this point marks the start of the Pennine Way. It is a delightful, primitive bridge, symbolic of all that the Pennine Way stands for—a simple, natural route striking northwards from Derbyshire for the 250 miles to Kirk Yetholm in Scotland.

The Youth Hostel at Rowland Cote might serve as base for the first night. From there a westward track leads to a little packhorse bridge at Grindsbrook at a point where the official National Park's Fieldhead Campsite has been established. Other campsites are to be found at local farms while a few cottages and the *Church Hotel* offer more substantial accommodation. The Fieldhead Campsite lies almost adjacent to the Church and just beyond these points and the *Nag's Head Inn*, a swift descent through a wooded glade brings us to the fallen tree.

With measured steps we cross the firm, broad back of the twenty foot span, thrilled with the prospect that must surely lie ahead, then up the stone steps to the stile above to turn left into pastures where sheep are brought down for the winter but now in summer,

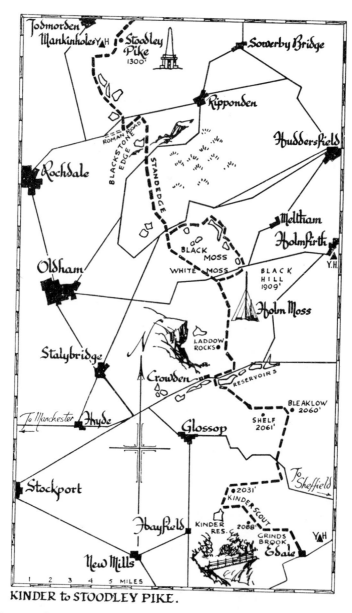

KINDER to STOODLEY PIKE.

There are hostels at Crowden and at Marsden, near Standedge. The hostel at Holmfirth is closed.

10

enlivened by the white flares of retreating rabbits. A further stile into a copse brings the further temptation to look back upon Edale — to see the skyline with Mam Tor separated by the nick of a road from the long ridge of Rushup Edge, or perhaps to contemplate the numerous footpath routes which abound. Through the wood, another stile, and we are thrust straight into the deep edge of Grindsbrook — the climb of Kinder has begun.

Typical of gritstone areas, the steep "V" shaped clough curves up towards the summit edge. The stream tumbles away on our left over a bed littered with boulders, and broken here and there by a pleasant fall with a pool below. The path gradually climbs, sometimes dry, often peaty and wet; following the stream until it degenerates into the stream bed itself, which becomes a great heap of tumbled boulders beneath the towering edge of Kinder.

It is a valley cloaked with bilberry, where decorative caterpillars of the Emperor Moth browse in summer months. On hot days, numerous heavy Dor Beetles and the smaller Minotaurs tumble about the turf or move laboriously across the path, while in contrast to these scavengers, the predatory Tiger Beetles, sparkling green and armed with powerful jaws, hunt their prey. In spite of the abundance of these and other forms of life, you will be more fascinated by the route through the great chaos of boulders that lies ahead.

Balancing, hopping, jumping from one block to another and enjoying simple climbs on the massive rocks, we may revel in our scramble, made infinitely more exhilarating by the surge of water beneath our feet. Near the top, the boulders give way to a pavement gorge swept clear of all debris by the occasional torrents that pour down. Gritstone pavements and steps, where erosion follows the course of tilted or almost horizontal bedding planes, form the remainder of our route to the summit edge, reached by a final neat step over an eight foot ledge. We are straight away made aware that Kinder is a plateau, for it suddenly levels out, and from here to the summit, over a mile away, is a rise of less than a 100 feet.

Dark oceans of peat rise and fall — giant breakers tipped with bilberry crowns — and through this fantasy world of peaty walls, the sandy course leads on towards the summit. Grindsbrook offers an easy route with the sheep track alongside. The peat acts as a sponge, absorbing water in heavy squalls and letting it out gradually so that the risk of flooding is very much reduced, while in times of drought the steady flow trickles into the streams which are only rarely dry. The water is soft and pure, and excellent for drinking, although it is necessary to add some lime for general supply since it is acid and would otherwise corrode supply pipes. The additional lime is also a health benefit in the water supply to neighbouring populations.

No matter where you cross Kinder, you inevitably come out on this plateau surface: a broad expanse of peaty waste with islands of cotton grass in a blue-black sea. Sometimes it is chocolate-brown and spongy, but more often than not, it is a black, sticky ooze.

Now head north-west and you come to a tributary which leads on to Kinder River, a great highway cutting across the summit; a highway of sand and quartz crystals and littered with gritstone boulders on the approach to Kinder Gates. Walking between Kinder Gates is like passing between two headlands on some foreshore, but instead of the sea in front, the river winds on in a series of curves until you come suddenly on the edge, and look out into space.

That is one of the great joys of Kinder. No matter where you come out on the edge, there it is—sharply defined!—and you can look out for miles. Perhaps it is hazy and you can just make out the form of Kinder Reservoir. If it is misty, those huge, great slabs seem to tumble away into space. Here too Kinder Downfall plunges a full 100 feet.

The Downfall varies from day to day. From a mere trickle over the ledge to a massive curtain plunging downwards. The two arms of Kinder stretching to the south and west usher in all the force of a south-west wind to that one point, so that if a strong south-westerly blows and the stream is in spate, the Downfall erupts as a geyser. On such days, a great feathery plume sways over the crest of Kinder as the water is plucked up in its path and is lashed furiously back over the summit edge in the force of a gale. It is visible for many miles and under such conditions even the Shelter Stone catches the full fury and those who usually enjoy this refuge have to seek shelter among the massive blocks on the far side, and there enjoy a rare spectacle of power and beauty.

Kinder has its moods, and each visit will leave new and varied impressions. You may climb through mist to stand on its summit edge in sparkling sun, an island above the clouds—the supreme joy of all hill country. More often, you will climb in clear air, only to be enveloped in cloud that makes the compass an essential companion. In a severe winter the Downfall is transformed into a cascade of glittering ice.

We move on from Kinder Downfall, following the clearly etched path along the edge to the north-west tip, there to descend to the head of William's Clough and take the slight rise to Mill Hill. Look back at Kinder from here, and you will see this great fortress with battlements extending away to the east and as far to the south.

Beyond Mill Hill, follow the watershed to Moss Castle even though it may meander. Short cuts across lower ground inevitably bring you into morass whereas the summit sheep track offers some relief from the stumbling tussocks of cotton grass on either side. After Moss Castle, the Snake Road is crossed at its highest point, 1,680 feet. This smooth highway connecting Glossop and Sheffield, contrasts strongly with the surface of the Pennine Way and the earlier Roman Road of Doctor's Gate, where weathered gritstone blocks bear testimony to the ravages of time. More recent erosion of a different kind, the heavy tread of well shod feet along the Pennine Way, has marked this route in trench-like fashion. To counteract this wear and tear an experimental plastic covered path now overlies a layer of heather brushwood compacted with the trough. It feels like walking on a floating bog except the feet keep reasonably dry. This plastic way is only a very short stretch at the peak erosion point connecting the Snake Road to just beyond the stile. For the purists there is a further stile close by which allows alternative access through the swampy peat and recent information indicates that the laminated plastic will soon be replaced by bundles of heather brushwood, a better alternative.

By Devil's Dyke and round the head of Crooked Clough, occasional boundary stakes mark out the watershed and make it easier to follow, but in bad visibility this is an exercise in navigation —the map, the compass and time. Shelf Moss is finally approached by following the source of Hern Clough through the great depth of peat which exceeds some fifteen feet. You will remember passing between these sombre walls. To be caught in mist without a compass on Bleaklow would be a considerably more difficult situation than a similar episode on Kinder. Kinder is a vast plateau flanked on all sides by roads or tracks. Bleaklow is a veritable maze of peat hags, steep gullies and extensive swamps. The wrong downhill course could lead to an exhausting trek, while it is easy to make circuits on the expansive summits without some directional aid. Bleaklow offers a good challenge even with the right knowledge and equipment. To be lacking in either of these is to court disaster. Without doubt, this is the wildest part of the whole of the Pennines.

The Pennine Way avoids the more savage parts and although no visible track offers guidance, there is no difficulty in crossing. The steady course is interrupted periodically by knee-deep swamps amongst the cotton grass and peat; diversions are inevitable until the final approach over easy ground of wasting peat to Wain Stones, the great boulders which dominate Bleaklow Head.

The moorland masses sprawl away as far as the eye can see, and to the north, across Longdendale, lies Black Hill, the highest point in Cheshire, with the 750 ft. pencil mast of Holme Moss Television Station on its shoulder. It is visible from Kinder on a clear day. On the north side, too, lies Torside Clough, the deepest cut into that side of Bleaklow, and this forms the next stage of our route. You may cross this strange, almost lunar landscape without trouble, but never consider Bleaklow with other than respect. Mistakes invariably lead to the wilderness of the "Swamp" and Hern Basin and thence to the tortuous and precipitous route of the Alport— exhilarating when taken by choice, but shattering when joined in error.

The great sweeping edge of the summit of Torside Clough offers splendid views of Longdendale, with the reservoirs, roads and railway laid out like miniatures below. At the bottom of the clough, the water speeds along its pavements, through narrow gorges, and plunges downwards over the familiar steps to the litter of boulders where a dam and embankment drain lead to the Swineshaw Reservoirs. Water gathering is a predominant use of all these moorlands, there being over two hundred reservoirs on the gritstone Pennines. The flanks of Longdendale are most jealously guarded by Manchester Corporation Waterworks.

The steep descent from the rim of Torside Clough brings you to Reaps, the first habitation since leaving Edale, some 15 miles and seven hours behind. From Torside Clough the eye will have followed the sweep of the railway line round to Crowden, from which point it runs alongside the Woodhead Reservoir and plunges into the three and a quarter-mile tunnel.

The old and ornate Woodhead Tunnels of the days of steam lie alongside the wide and illuminated bore of the new tunnel constructed for the electrification of the line. The entrances to the former are now bricked up, but one of the tunnels is now used as an underground route of cables of the National Grid and the massive pylons congregate around the entrance in an overpowering array. The splendour of the former scene is now dwarfed beneath this cavalcade which strides the full length of the valley. The Pennine Way passes beneath the cables and by the Torside level crossing leads on to the dam of Torside Reservoir, at which point we leave Derbyshire and enter Cheshire.

Longdendale is bleak and austere, although at one time squirrels could leap from branch to branch all the way from the lower valley up to Woodhead. Now the hillsides are bare save for a few sheltered spots and meagre plantations. A combination of factors; the heavy rainfall and leaching of the soil, the encroachment of acid peat, and the ravages of the wind seem to underly this facade of tortuous, twisted branches and shattered trunks that screen the landslips on the south side of Longdendale. Nor can the cooling effect of the reservoirs be entirely discounted in this change. It is the contrast with Edale, so green and luxuriant, yet only a few miles to the south and at a similar height, that is so striking. Edale is sheltered from all sides by high ground. Longdendale lies open to the south-west wind and all that goes with it.

The few folk who live in Longdendale have become fewer for they have to battle not only with the elements, but with the changes of our economy. That great meeting place, the *George and Dragon Inn*, held its last open house on the evening of January 8th, 1961 when over 150 people were there for the wake, singing "John Peel" and "Ilkley Moor" and telling almost legendary tales of the inn which was overlooking the Woodhead Reservoir and was closed by Manchester's Waterworks Committee as part of the policy of restricting human habitations within the drainage areas.

The late landlord, Eddie Bagshaw, is remembered with great affection. His high pitched voice and outstretched hand welcomed all, and many a traveller must have enjoyed a mug of tea or something stronger alongside his roaring peat fire in winter. Annie, his wife, recounted tales of winters when snowdrifts were so deep around the inn that it was possible to feed rabbits from the bedroom windows. On occasions the *George and Dragon Inn* has provided refuge for up to forty stranded drivers for nearly a week. They slept on the floor and on any conceivable surface. She recalled too, a winter when a party of soldiers came over from the railway line. When asked how they had come, they said "Over the fields down there". They had crossed over the 60 ft. deep reservoir cloaked with ice and snow.

Now all this has gone, and the cold wind blows across this once hospitable place. But all is not lost — the rich memories of friendships with shepherds, watermen, gamekeepers, railmen and travellers are still a nourishing source of joy, and a new meeting place has now been created in the establishment of the Hostel at Crowden.

A row of cottages at Crowden has been modernised and transformed into the Peak National Park Hostel. This is open to Youth Hostel members and non members alike, although the former pay reduced rates. As well as dormitory accommodation, private single or double rooms are also available, while meals or supplies are provided at request. There can be no more welcome sight than this pleasing hostel exactly on the route after the arduous crossing of Kinder and Bleaklow, or even the moorland to the north if walking in the reverse direction. Prior to this, the nearest hostel was at Holmfirth or else you had to climb well clear of the drainage area to establish a few tents on Standedge or neighbouring summits.

On the approach to the hostel, the route passes through grazing land connected with the Quiet Shepherd. The name springs from an old inn and not from the sheep-rearing with which Mr. Hawksworth is concerned. The main breeds in these parts are the Scottish Blackface and the Derbyshire Gritstone, and in general the farms are very extensive, for the grazing land is the open moor which offers some fescue grass on the lower slopes but poor stuff on the higher ground.

All the farms work within the framework of restrictions laid down by the waterworks to protect the purity of supply. Out of some 2,400 acres a neighbouring farm only has about 20 acres for hay. Ploughing and other treatments of the soil which are routine on other farms are strictly controlled in this area, and apart from the individual need of the farmer, cattle are prohibited. However, the shepherds are primarily concerned with their sheep and, because of the limited numbers, probably know their animals better than most. This is particularly true at Pikenaze Farm where, as a lad, young Rider Howard not only knew each one of his eight hundred sheep, but could pick out the parentage.

In 1952 the proposed route followed the course of Crowden Brook, and by chance, as we paused to drink by the stream the local gamekeeper came upon us. We were told that we had no right to be there so we sported the Ramblers' Association Route

Guide. However, the Pennine Way had not at that time been opened, and we received new instructions. "The Way runs on the tops, and not by the brook", we were informed by the keeper who stayed to observe our progress to the foot of Laddow Rocks.

It seems odd that access to these watercourses should cause such constant concern to the Manchester Waterworks when roads and a railway run alongside the main reservoir at Woodhead. The chance of pollution by ramblers is extremely small, and although we agree that anything to the detriment of the community must be avoided, we cannot help thinking that it is a greater detriment to general health to bar the freedom of the moors.

Economically, these moorlands represent water gathering grounds, supplying one-third of Manchester's needs, and they support a controlled amount of sheep rearing. They are also major recreational areas for the heavily populated towns and cities which lie close to the foothills. Below Laddow Rocks is the Crowden Shooting Range, now converted to an Outdoor Pursuits Centre. The only shooting these days is indicated by the lines of shooting butts which are a potent reminder of the Glorious Twelfth. Grouse shooting is a highly organised affair, and with all the associated protection given to the birds throughout the rest of the year, together with the preservation of the moor, enables a much higher population of grouse to be maintained than would otherwise be possible. The red grouse is a splendid bird, our only true native, and its call, "Go back, go back, go back," will be heard many times on the way.

Laddow Rocks offer a 100 ft. gritstone face, and provide some of the finest climbs in Cheshire, but whether you ascend by the skilled and exhilarating routes of the climber, or footslog round the side, the reward at the top is just the same: the thrill of looking out across a vast gulf with some dark, overhanging crag in the fore. Both rocks and moorland are scoured and blackened by an atmosphere polluted by the sooty rain: the product of a ring of towns weeping from the skies. This will change with the new era of smokeless zones, but it will take many years and the sombre nature of the rocks will continue to hold that strange fascination that will draw you many times to these moors.

To the north the moorland sprawls away. Go over one great horizon, and there is another, just as big and vast, and just as far away—"Featherbed Moss"—the white down of cotton grass confirming the name. Thus we proceed on to Black Hill, the highest point in Cheshire, 1,908 feet above sea level, with the mast of the television station balancing on its pencil point and towering some 750 feet above the shoulder, and we plod now across the flattened dome in the wake of a storm. "Black Hill" is wonderfully named, the blackness intensified by the rain-sodden peat and the swirling mist. The atmosphere of the moors is conveyed in a manner not likely to be forgotten: shapeless mounds of wasting peat, vague outlines, and shadowy figures impressed on the mind while working on compass through the dark scene.

Since my first crossing, the route from Crowden has been altered to follow the east side of Crowden Little Brook by Hey Moss, Westend Moss and Tooleyshaw Moss to Black Hill. The track is clearly marked in the early stages by signposts erected by the Manchester Corporation Waterworks, and although it holds regrets for those who love to follow streams, it has its compensations. The drainage clefts within the peat of Westend Moss display the tree roots of old forests which once covered this terrain, and give further confirmation of another world of not too distant past. The R.A. official route however, still follows Crowden Great Brook, whereas the current O.S. tourist map marks the route via Hey Moss. The new 50000 Map once again confirms the original R.A. route.

Beyond Black Hill, the Pennine Way offers an alternative low-level route for bad weather, cutting downhill (north-east) by the head of Hey Clough before turning N.N.E. to follow the straight boundary ditch leading to the A635 Holmfirth road to Wessenden Head. A clearly marked track leads just beyond the road by the Wessenden Valley.

About 600 yards below the Wessenden Reservoir take the footbridge across the stream to ascend the clough and then head westwards across undefined moorland to reach the main route at the south-east corner of the high reservoir, and thence N.W. to Standedge. Those who take this alternative route will be interested to hear of the experience of one walker, John Lawson, who found his best overnight stay along the whole of the route at the *Coach and Horses Hotel*, Marsden, where the hotelier not only made his group of ramblers welcome, but transported them to their starting point on the following morning. Those who plan to use Youth Hostel accommodation will be pleased to learn of the new hostel at Marsden (the former Co-op) which opened in July, 1975.

The main route from Black Hill, however, is an undefined trail across the interminable peat bogs of Wessenden Head Moor, following the watershed N.W. to cross the A635 Saddleworth-Holmfirth road at its highest point 1,615 feet. The area on both sides of this road was the scene of the search for bodies in the appalling "Moors Murder Case" and the Pennine Way walker will not fail to be impressed by the ability of the police in finding anything at all from this overwhelming morass.

The peat along these tracts is as deep as anywhere in the Pennines and the names "White Moss" and "Black Moss" refer to the cotton grass "mosses"; cotton grass growing only where the rainfall is forty-five inches or more. All this is emphasised by the squelching feet and unstable tussocks which reduce walking speed to a mere two miles an hour. If you stray from the watershed, you are rewarded with an obstacle course second to none! Such is the way to Standedge.

Standedge is about as far — 23 miles — as a really strenuous party carrying camping equipment would make in one day from Edale. My groups have invariably called it a day near the summit of Black Hill if they have not already made use of the hostel at Crowden or camped on the army site nearby. No doubt there are some who would do more, but the prospect of a good site at Standedge Cutting is worth aiming for. Do not, however, underestimate your food requirements (including emeregency reserve). A number of parties have regretted not buying food supplies early in the day. This is one of the basic lessons of the Pennine Way.

Day 2: Standedge to Hebden Bridge via Stoodley Pike

22 miles from Crowden; 15 miles from Standedge. Total 37 miles.

O.S. 1:50 000 Map Series Sheets 110; 109 and 103. The 1:25 000 Outdoor Leisure Map, "South Pennines", covers the route from the crossing of M62 to well north of Hebden Bridge.

Walking speed estimate 2 m.p.h. (carrying packs).

This stage and the last are linked more loosely than most since, unless you stay at Crowden, it is better to aim at splitting these two first very strenuous days into almost equal parts. In the whole of the first thirty-five miles you will pass very few habitations and the only source of food will be Crowden Hostel (15 miles) with possible extras at the *White House Inn* (30 miles) unless you make the diversion to Marsden.

Beyond Standedge we follow the crest of the moor overlooking the steep western slopes with the reservoirs and industrial fingers way below. In contrast to the sodden turf and mounds of cotton grass mosses, the moors tend to be better drained and support a vegetation of heather, heath, bilberry and the like. This is apparent as we follow the watershed from White Hill (1,533 ft.) along the ridge of Bleakedgate Moor. Blackstone Edge is in sight as we cross the A672 Halifax road alongside the television reflector station on Windy Hill. But it is not the dark outline of Blackstone Edge or the pylon-like mast of the radio station which will strike you most at this point; it is here that the air resounds to the whine and roar of speeding cars and lorries as the Pennine Way crosses the Lancashire/Yorkshire Motorway, M62, by the slender arch of a high level footbridge.

Great slabs of rock mark Blackstone Edge. Jumbled, disorderly heaps build gradually into a rough and weathered escarpment, below which huge blocks lie tilted in all directions, half buried in peat and sand. Distant reservoirs gleam in the sun, and to the north we join the Roman Road at Aiggin Stone and wander down the heavy cobbles of this ancient track. The blocks are in good order, particularly near the crossing of the embankment drain, which we follow by its contour route to the A58 just below the *White House Inn*.

We finish the day by the pleasant, easy track which skirts the reservoirs and regulating drain to the north, and brings us by a rigorous moorland stretch to Stoodley Pike. We might stay at the Youth Hostel of Mankinholes below or camp on the summit to enjoy the fascinating sparkle of the distant lights and the strings of amber that connect the towns. (A tiny stream on the north slope provides water).

This is a welcome respite after the laborious trek over interminable "mosses", where one vast horizon merged with another as we scrambled and squelched our way north from Black Hill. Nor have we finished with our sodden gritstone moors. Stoodley Pike is a firm reminder for those who spend the night at Mankinholes. Although a dwarf compared with the previous peaks, the steep slopes offer good early morning exercise and a few extra feet can be climbed up the staircase within the massive walls of the monument. Built originally to commemorate the Battle of Waterloo, it was destroyed by lightning on the outbreak of the Crimean War and later rebuilt in similar form with the balcony from which to view the ever-changing scene.

Two miles of steady descent brings us to the towering four-storey houses, stern terraces moulded from and within the sombre, precipitous valley. Water streams down the gritstone walls and along pavements deserted by all save those who have to be out in the rain. Beyond the thick walls is the warmth of glowing fires, while the outer world of greyish stone echoes the clatter of heels on wet flags. Canal, railway, river and road lie side by side in this clustered ribbon of the industrial revolution. This is Hebden Bridge, stark monument to West Riding tradition. It is changing. Houses are being pulled down and new building takes place, but there is still plenty of the old town to give the atmosphere of another age. Of more immediate concern to the Pennine Way walker, the many shops, catering and residential establishments will more than meet his needs.

Such are the first 37 miles — toil and rigour; dark and sombre crags; endless peats and "mosses" and the most memorable experiences.

Day 3: Hebden Bridge to Lothersdale

O.S. 1: 50 000 Map Series Sheet 103. The new 1: 25 000 Outdoor Leisure Map, "South Pennines", covers the route from Hebden Bridge to Ickornshaw Moor, near Ponden (east of Colne).

17 miles.   **Total 54 miles.**

Walking Speed—2 m.p.h. to beyond Heptonstall Moor (4 miles) and 3 m.p.h. thereafter (13 miles).

A steep, stone flagged track climbs from under the railway bridge and leads to the marginal farmland above. Below us, the close-packed town is concealed by the steepness of the hillside and as we ascend, the view opens out to embrace the distant hills and the sky. Stoodley Pike, a faint grey outline, lies to the south. To the north is the open moor — and a brighter sky.

Heptonstall Moor, shallow peat with heather at first, develops into a morass of mat grass, making walking difficult. Drainage channels have been cut and where these lie in the right direction it is easier to follow them than plod a straight line across the moor. Sheep tracks too make the going a little easier. It is almost as if in that next hour we walk out of a veil of cloud and mist and smoke, away from the areas of industrial pollution, and out into the clear air of the north, into a new type of landscape. The sides of the valleys become shallow and smoothed in contrast to the steep declivities to which we have become accustomed. Heather is in bloom and the cotton grass and fescues lie burnished by the sun. It was in the habitations of these parts that John Wesley raised a strong following; the first Methodist chapel is to be seen at Heptonstall.

Beyond the Widdop road near the *Pack Horse Inn* — you might here enjoy food and a welcome from landlord Ted Harrison — the track leads northwards along the stream to the Walshaw Dean (Halifax) reservoirs. Between the two reservoirs stands the Waterman's House, its gritstone walls glowing with a warmth of colour that is lost on the blackened buildings further south. This walk along the dam and eastern watercourse of the reservoir is pleasant underfoot

20

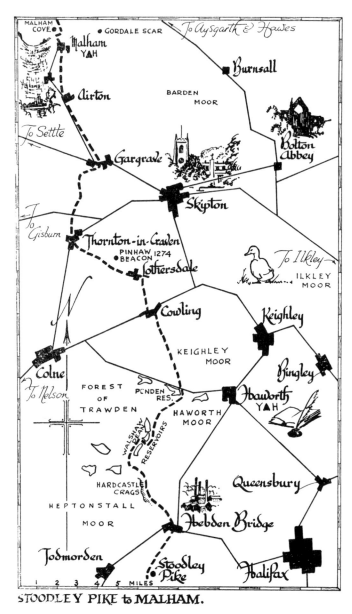

STOODLEY PIKE to MALHAM.

There are hostels at Earby, between Colne and Thornton-in-Craven, and at Haworth.

after all the hobbling over uncertain mounds of matted grasses which have characterised much of the previous terrain.

It is a joy to amble along and admire the purples, russets and greens in the surrounding hills, while the water reflects the brilliance of the sun when we look back along the way we have come. The smoothed and rounded rhododendron bushes along the embankment are pruned, not by man, but by the wind. Any buds exposed to the severe winds are killed by the drying and cooling so that growth tends to be in a gradually flattened plane, rather like an upturned saucer. Any shoots which grow out from this self-protected area are desiccated by the elements.

The wind is a powerful force in shaping life on the moors. It carves the rocks with the sand it carries. It dries and it kills. To escape it, plants grow in mat or carpet formation, or even lie prostrate in submission, and their leaves may be dwarfed, waxy or needle-shaped, or all of these to reduce this desiccation. We know from personal experience the chilling action of a wind, and for every hill walker the secret of warmth lies not in many layers of heavy clothing, but in having a good windproof on the outside.

I well remember, on my first Pennine journey, the footpath to Withins Height, clearly visible and marked with neat, unobtrusive signposts, and fairly dry in spite of the rain of previous days. Here was the background to Emily Brontë's "Wuthering Heights", a background of gloom and desolation transformed by the sun and a blue sky into a serene moorland setting. We were in luck!—the sun warmed our backs as we headed towards Ponden. Yet before we had covered that short span of moor, the towering nimbus had spread its anvil shape across our path and, within its shadow, the wind freshened to a sudden squall, the prelude to a thunder shower. We crouched alongside a gritstone wall enjoying the spray and vibrant tattoo upon our capes as sheets of water loosed upon us, while with each startling flash came the crack and boom of nearby thunder. It stopped as quickly as it started, and even before the shadow moved on, a shaft from the sun broke forth with double its former resplendence. The moor glistened and sparkled with water, each diamond blade of grass bent low. All the while the double rainbows glowed against the blackness of a monsoon sky. Slowly they drifted away, leaving behind the fields of burnished gold.

Top Withins still stands, a roofless ruin by a windswept tree, a mecca for photographers, artists and Brontë followers alike, enhanced by dramatic skies and weather that all too frequently more than convey the scene. It is thus with great satisfaction that we descend by Master Stones to skirt Ponden Reservoir and take the clearly marked tracks which lead north to Cowling and to Lothersdale. An alternative route would be to make a three mile detour from Ponden to Haworth where there is no lack of accommodation or supplies. Haworth offers much to enthral those who enjoy the settings of the early industrial age. The Parsonage, home of the Brontë sisters, is preserved as a living museum. The tiny dresses of the sisters, with other personal belongings, re-create their frail and tragic lives.

Gritstone houses, steeply cobbled streets and vintage lamps enhance the old world image, while down at the station, particularly at weekends, the age of steam lives on. The Keighley and Worth Valley Railway not only displays a fine array of vintage stock and locomotives: it runs them! Shrill whistles, and the pounding, rhythmic beat of steam resound across the valley, as they have done for a century, and will do, I trust, for centuries to come. All is not lost! Haworth well repays a visit.

The new Youth Hostel which opened in Haworth is an ideal centre for those who have the time to make this minor diversion from the route. The new 50000 O.S. Map Sheet 104 (Leeds and Bradford) covers this area. (Old O.S. Map Sheet 96.)

Continuing along the direct Pennine Way route, accommodation or a campsite may be found at Woodhead Farm, just before entering Lothersdale. Walkers will find a very real welcome here.

Youth hostellers still have some way to go in order to reach the next hostel which lies at Earby. In this case, the Pennine Way is followed by Pinhaw Beacon and to Elslack Moor before branching off from the steady north-west heading to Thornton-in-Craven. (Hostel a further 3½ miles, from Lothersdale.)

Day 4:   Lothersdale to Malham

The 1: 25 000 Outdoor Leisure Map, "Malham and Upper Wharfedale", covers the route from Gargrave to Malham.
16 miles   Total 70 miles.
Good footpaths—walking speed 3 m.p.h.

Mile upon mile, in sun or in rain, the countryside gradually unfolds before us. The moorlands recede, and we meander by hedgerows and pasture of marginal farmland. Our track crosses the amazing flow of the drumlins which lie in shape and posture as a shoal of "great leviathans" beached and stranded as they swam, and now the sweeping contours of these hills reveal the trail of glacial flows. We stand astride one such whaleback, as we cross from Thornton-in-Craven to the Leeds and Liverpool Canal.

This is a colourful stretch in the sun, the canal weaving through the drumlin trail, curving gently first this way and then by cutting or embankment across to the next. Under the double bridge of East Marton then away from the canal we pass by Great Meadow Plantation. A few drooping willows by the stream are the only confirmation of this name as our path by stiles and fencing leads to Gargrave, the Yorkshire village on the banks of the river Aire. In sunshine, we enjoy the picturesque beauty of its cottages and the setting astride the river. A fine bridge spans the Aire, but I recall how my young charges found something better, the stepping stones. They were aptly called the "buttertubs."

Gargrave is a good spot for refreshment and supplies, after which the trail leads on to the north: a pleasant footpath threading between good pasture and arable land before re-joining the Aire about a mile south of Airton. This crossing of Eshton Moor is sometimes a little tricky, but the distinctive little woods are a clear guide to your position. The final descent to the Aire is clearly marked and from there to Malham, the route follows the banks of the stream. Between Hanlith and Malham the official route goes along the east bank of the river. There is a parallel route on the western bank which skirts behind Scale Gill Mill.

Make a point of visiting Malham if you have not already done so. The village itself is pleasant enough, but add to it the splendours of the Cove and Janet's Foss, together with Gordale Scar, and you will still find more to enthral you. Malham has its roots deep in the past. Prehistoric men roamed the upper moor, where their flint implements may still be found, while the Bronze Age stone circle at Bordley and the burial mounds and village sites of Iron Age are other archaeological interests. Most of the villages of Malhamdale were established about the sixth century and hoard a wealth of historical detail. Yet we can go back much further than this, for Malham is built on limestone, a rock containing the fossiliferous remains of creatures that were alive some three hundred million years ago in a clear limestone sea. The two hills, Cawden and Wedber, are reef knolls and specimen corals and brachiopods (shells) may be chipped from the rock. The remnants of a tumbled wall on Wedber (near Janet's Foss) contained numerous fossils but many have been removed by collectors.

From the crest of Farleygate Lane, leading to Gordale, the sudden change from the sombre fawns and browns of the gritstone country-side to the brighter landscape of the limestone is apparent. This is the Mid-Craven Fault marking a great dislocation of rock strata, the older limestone rocks lying exposed to the north. It is the change of vegetation from one rock to the other that makes the contrast so distinctive, for the acid, peaty soils of the gritstones and shales bear a coarse vegetation of matted grasses, heather, bilberry and bracken, none of which will be found growing on the sweeter soils of the lime.

Gordale Scar emphasises even more dramatically the change in scene, for the vertical limestone walls are quite unlike any aspect found on the grits. The sides rise steeply, displaying screes which originate from the crags above, while down in the bottom, Gordale Beck swells rapidly as a number of underground springs discharge into it. The beck has two main tributaries, one denuded of all plant life by the lime deposits (tufa) while the other displays a profusion of watercress. Beyond this point, the valley closes to a narrow ravine with Cyclopean walls which tower on either side for 300 feet. It is either a collapsed cave or pothole laid open to the sky, or else a fantastic outflow channel scoured out beneath the ice by meltwaters of a bygone age.

Down the centre of the gorge Gordale Beck plunges in two great falls. The upper fall issues from a cave over a tongue of tufa formed like the one at Janet's Foss, upon once growing mosses, while the lower fall tumbles across the full width of the gorge. The water roars and sprays in the exhilarating climb to the top, where we leap the foaming torrent to the loose scree slopes. The rocky arch still higher, disgorges the beck as one precipitous fall, shattering in spray before tumbling downwards the way we have come. In winter I have seen the upper fall as a great tongue of ice, up which expert snow and ice climbers ascend with the aid of ice pitons.

From the scree, we may climb the great rocky buttress which rears like a knife-edge ridge. Views from the summit will not be forgotten as you gaze into the chasm. Down below, the turbulent water speeds through its gorge and into the cave arch before hurtling outwards into the lower abyss. Upstream, great crags stand on either side of the beck, a strange uncanny scene like a world of the past, but instead of some monster lumbering round the corner, only the jackdaws wheel and cry "Jack! Jack! Jack!" Should we wish, we could follow the beck to the summit of the moor and Malham Tarn. Such is Gordale Scar, an inspiration, a challenge, and a highlight in our adventure along the Pennine Way.

To scramble and enjoy the grandeur of Gordale Scar and wander by Janet's Foss, with its elfin cave and the waterfall fanning out in delicate tracery across the rocks, is only part of the attraction of Malham. Further along the Pennine Way, the Cove is still to be explored and beyond that, the Tarn.

If there is any place along our route which justifies an extra day, then this is it. It has its full share of amenities from simple cafés, a post office and stores, to the splendid Youth Hostel or more stately places should you care to stay. Beck Hall offers antique surroundings, old world comfort and the pleasant company of Bill Hardaker, a figure well known in the scouting world and who enjoys opening up his places for the benefit of young parties. For campers, Mr. Moon of Townhead Farm will supply a site in a field near the Cove. Tents look well in this field which is ridged by Iron Age field boundaries, but those who use them should respect the country code and leave no trace.

Do not underestimate this journey. If you have accomplished this first 70 miles in the four days outlined, you may feel assured that you will almost certainly cover the rest on schedule, or even finish ahead of our 16 days, but there are still some hard days to come, and there will be a sting at the tail!

Day 5: Malham to Horton-in-Ribblesdale

1:50 000 Map Series   Sheet 98, or the 1:25 000 Outdoor Leisure Map, "Malham and Upper Wharfedale".
15 miles   **Total 85 miles.**
Two main ascents—walking speed 2 m.p.h.

Malham Cove, a great amphitheatre set back in the limestone hillside, forms an impressive start to the next stage of our Pennine Journey. Regular mounds of rock in the near field are remnants of Iron Age field boundaries, while the evidence of cultivation from a thousand years ago is to be seen in the lynchets, terraces etched into the far hillside and fretted by the unique array of enclosure walls. You might not see these things unless you look for them, for the eye is continually drawn to the Cove, to the very setting that inspired Kingsley when he wrote *The Water Babies*. That dark streak down the rock face was made by the chimney sweep boys as they slipped into the underwater kingdom, for this was the background to the scene.

The immensity of the Cove is more apparent as you approach and see the ash trees dwarfed by mighty terraces, too large to be absorbed by the eye at once. You might care to traverse the lower terrace. It is an easy route and gives the best impression of the vastness of this wall, soaring skywards to the summit ledge — a great mantelshelf which shelters martins' nests, from which the tiny birds dart out and fly in circles.

The notch on the upper lip marks the point where at one time in the past, water used to plunge, but it is over 200 years since the water was last recorded over this 300 ft. edge, and nowadays the water is swallowed underground long before it reaches this point. Malham Beck, which issues from a broad crevice at the foot of this wall, might appear to be the water which once plunged from the summit, but this is not so. In fact, the water which emerges is swallowed high on Malham Moor near the ruins of an old smelt mill, whereas the stream from Malham Tarn which is swallowed up on the approach to the Cove, appears again some distance below Malham at the Aire Head Springs. All these tributaries, together with Gordale Beck, form the headwaters of the river Aire which we first encountered at Gargrave.

At the top of the Cove, a stile in the limestone wall gives access to the summit and our first introduction to the limestone pavements, the clints and the grikes. The clints are the pavements, the grikes the channels in between — deep, vertical joints which have been dissolved by the action of rainwater which is slightly acid. The surface of the rock is fissured into a maze of drainage channels by this same action, for limestone is a soluble rock. Some large blocks have been completely eroded from the main and they tilt under your feet, as you step from one to another. Between them, deep in their crevices, a rich variety of plants thrives in security against the grazing of animals. We balance from one clint to the next, rock an occasional block, and keep clear of the very edge of the Cove, for to tilt a block here might be tipping the scales a little too far. When it is wet, however, the rock can be treacherously slippery.

Above the Cove lies the dry limestone valley excavated by the glacial torrents of a bygone age, with evidence of another waterfall carved into the wild, spectacular scene at the head of the valley. But our route skirts the deep cleft and joins it higher in its course at a point marked on the map as "Water Sinks". This describes exactly what happens. A stream outlet from Malham Tarn, flows along the ground and disappears through limestone rubble adjacent to the wall. It is the initial stage in the formation of a pothole, and from that point, the water pursues the underground course destined to emerge at Aire Head Springs.

There are numerous sink holes along this tract of country, marking the line where the impervious Silurian shales come into contact with the limestone at the North Craven Fault, a change reflected, too, in the contrasting vegetation. These shales support Malham Tarn which has the distinction of being the highest lake in the Pennines, 1,229 ft. above sea level. The Tarn stretches into view shortly afterwards, its span of a good half mile across being partly concealed by a belt of trees whose margins are torn by exposure. Its northern shore is overlooked by Tarn House, the noted Field Centre, where one might enjoy the company of naturalists and experts in other fields who seek to explore and make known still more of the fascinating story of Malham.

Fountains Fell looms ahead, approached by way of Tennant Gill, which is generally dry in spite of the rain of previous days. The climb follows an old mine track which rapidly becomes unrecognisable as we come upon the coarser tufted grasses and rushes of higher ground. Here again is that transition from limestone to grits and shales, the change from a fine limestone turf to the tussocky, matted growths of an acid gritstone moor. It is a story repeated time and time again along the Pennine Way, for the gritstone lies like a cap upon the lime, and you climb from one to another in the continued sequence of a theme, but with infinite variations.

Fountains Fell, connected still by name to that Abbey, adds much pleasure to our journey. As you make for the top, look back to see the splendid view of Malham Tarn and the hills beyond. Your greatest thrill lies ahead however as the horizon dips and you come face to face with Penyghent. Thus we view this "Queen of the Peaks" for the first time on our northern way. Its only rival in all the Pennines is neighbouring Ingleborough Hill.

The route now swings round the north side of Fountains Fell to make the steady descent to Peter Castle and Dale Head Farm. Here are classic views of Penyghent, which rears with startling beauty from the moor. But let us pause a while to look down Churn Milk Hole, and possibly descend this funnel-shaped shaft to see the fossils laid below. Spirifera shells and others lie tumbled by the score. Emerging from Churn Milk Hole, we turn again towards our peak with its mighty buttress terraces dropping steeply down towards our feet. The Way sweeps on and up this face, a good stiff climb of boulder slope and gritstone steps, a joyful scramble to a dominant ledge, and there, a smoothly rounded dome leads on towards the summit.

Fountains Fell now dominates the southern scene, but the attraction, as ever, lies with our route to the north. Down below, a slight pall of smoke marks the lime quarries at Horton. Beyond, rising gracefully from the limestone pavements, stands the sister peak of Ingleborough, splendid in its isolation. There too, hidden on the lower slopes of the distant hill is Gaping Gill. On my first Pennine journey there was a buzz of excitement in the prospect of a diversion to descend the great pot on the following day.

Down the northern flank of Penyghent we reach again the limestone with the fascination of its caves and pot holes, the dry valleys and extensive flora. Two pots lie on our route, although many others may be found in the surrounding countryside. Hunt Pot, a narrow rift into which the beck sprays, looks slippery, green and ominous, and drops ninety feet into the black depths. Well clear of the pot, fossils abound in the high ledges where the beck splashes down from the moor. A little further on, Hull Pot, large and very receptive, looks in comparison positively inviting. The beck is usually dry, but the stains on the rock show that in spate it still shoots its burden into the pit below. A stream from a cave at the foot of the pot some 60 ft. below the rim bursts out as a waterfall which is quickly swallowed by some other subterranean passage. Mr. Jackson of Douk Ghyll Farm, once told me that on occasions the whole pot has filled after a storm, and then emptied like a sink.

A walled track meanders down towards Horton-in-Ribblesdale. Although attracted by your destination, you will still find Penyghent holding your attention. Look before you leave the moor to see the "lion with paws outstretched", the bold outline that has stirred many a heart. From Horton-in-Ribblesdale she still commands the scene, framed now behind the contours of the church. In the walls surrounding the church can be seen the limestone and the grit emphasising once again that this is, indeed, the countryside of two rocks.

The trek from Malham is strenuous and the great pint pots of coffee or tea at the *Penyghent Café* are now almost a tradition. Peter and Joyce Bayes who run the place are enthusiastic about the Pennine Way and go out of their way to provide a service that will be remembered. All are welcome and Pennine Way walkers are sure to be invited to sign the log which by now has become quite impressive. The availability of lightweight expedition foods of considerable variety is a further help to those who are cooking their own meals on the journey. Information on campsites around Horton-in-Ribblesdale is always available from the store.

Other accommodation is available at the *Crown Hotel*, while the nearest Youth Hostel is at Stainforth. The splendid waterfalls at Stainforth Foss, with the swimming pools below (35 ft. and 15 ft. deep) make the extra few miles to this spot worthwhile.

Day 6: Horton-in-Ribblesdale to Hawes

O.S. 1:50 000 Map Series Sheet 98, or 1:25 000 Outdoor Leisure Map "The Three Peaks".
13 miles.   **Total 98 miles.**
An easy day—walking speed 3 m.p.h.

Leaving Horton we take a track alongside the *Crown Inn* (marked on the map as *New Inn*) and climb between the gritstone walls, an easy way which contours out beyond Sell Gill Barn and sweeps across brown, tinted moorland tracks towards Birkwith Moor. We swing to the west to pass the barn near Old Ing and make our way to the farmstead and the track which skirts Cave Hill.

Calf Holes lie just over the wall, a double chasm where the stream tumbles from the far rim in a 35 ft. drop to the stream below. Higher upstream is another fossil bed similar to that observed at Churn Milk Hole, but the main interest here lies in the open pot. A ladder descent to the pool would open up another world with a roomy passage downstream from the fall, knee-deep in water and eventually penetrating a maze of bedding planes, dry if you discount the mud. There is a concealed passage which leads by crawls and a very tight squeeze to the Brow Gill Cave system, the latter involving a climb down a narrow rift before giving access to the open moor. The passage upstream from the pot passes under the fall. It is low and narrow, but a broad shelf on the left displays such an array of straw stalactites that I count it as one of the most delightful passages that I have ever seen. Row after row, these white slender straws provide a spectacle of static crystalline beauty as we inch our way onwards to the final chamber where a 30 ft. waterfall tumbles down towards us.

However our way lies across the tops, turning now to cross Cam Beck above the great ravine, a deep rift with massive steps dropping to a gulf below, with tenacious trees swaying on its brim and massing in its depths. The Roman Road climbs steadily up the long spur towards Dodd Fell. To the right, the sickle arc of Oughtershaw cuts a shallow cleft, forsaken and remote. This is a true watershed of the Pennines, Oughtershaw flowing eastwards to the North Sea, while on our left, the Ribble and its tributaries flow westwards to the Irish Sea. Behind us now, the Ribblehead viaduct gracefully spans the moor. Beyond it towers the summit of Ingleborough, set against the backcloth of the shimmering sea at Morecambe.

No true description of our journey can leave this peak unmentioned. If Penyghent has any rival, this surely is the one. On my first journey along the Pennine Way we chose to add this as an extra spice both for its own indomitable beauty, and the chance of descending Gaping Gill. We had spent the night at the Stainforth Youth Hostel where a change and hot meal put us in good heart for an evening stroll. We were conscious of our lightness in walking without rucksacks and thoroughly enjoyed the crimson beauty of our first Pennine sunset. With such a blaze of colour we were confident that the next day would be fine. Of course, we were wrong! The morning greeted us with a steady drizzle which offered no prospect beyond a further increase, but as this was the day chosen to spend some time underground, we were not unduly perturbed. Arrangements had been made for the descent of Gaping Gill.

At the crescent-shaped depression of Bar Pot I recalled how the previous May I had been fortunate enough to join a party of the Midland Association of Mountaineers who descended it as an alternative way into the Gaping Gill system. The first descent of this route was made in 1949 by the British Speleological Association. Few moments in any exploration could be as singularly thrilling as the instant when the confinement of the passage leading from the bottom of Bar Pot opened into the vastness of the Main Chamber of Gaping Gill. A great shaft of light from the high, arched roof penetrated the darkness in which was draped a curtain foiled in luminous spray. Stirred by some breeze it swayed and shimmered, a great bridal train enlivened by the plunging comet heads of water.

It seemed odd that we should have to go so deep underground to see the highest unbroken waterfall in the country. The massive chamber is over 450 ft. long soaring a hundred and sixty feet to the roof. It is large enough to accommodate a good-sized building, and still have ample room to walk around. The great shaft rises for 365 ft. above the floor of the cave to reach the moorland above. Yet this is only part of the Gaping Gill system. There are over three miles of passages ramifying in all directions, some, large and roomy, skirting large pots; others in contrast, lowering to squalid mud crawls. Hensler's Passage is almost 500 yards long and at the most some 18 inches in height. There are caverns, too, which are decorated with ornate formations that delight the human eye — the cascades of stalactites and other crystal adornments which have a beauty of their own in the rightful setting of a cave.

These memories were brought to mind as we passed Bar Pot on that August day, and shortly afterwards our attention was focused on the mouth of Gaping Gill, set deep in a steep-sided funnel. Standing on the lip of the shaft, you can watch the water of Fell Beck plunge over the rim and spiral downwards until it disappears from sight into a black void. There is a certain primitive fear associated with something black and unknown; a chill feeling of horror that attends, looking down an abyss that has no visible bottom. Such feelings rapidly disperse with the understanding of the nature of things and, in the capable hands of the British Speleological Association, we had no qualms about the descent. If the boys had any, they were skilfully hidden, and all made the return journey with abounding enthusiasm.

A bridge had been fixed across the shaft and the water of Fell Beck diverted so that the main ledge was comparatively dry. The club members were encamped upstream, while adjacent to the pot, and protected by a canopy, was the engine which operated the winch. The cable would support three tons, and thus reassured, we crossed the bridge to the chair, and once seated, were chained to it. There was no escape, the descent had begun!

The first few feet required some holding off, but beyond that the chair moved outwards to the centre of the shaft and was guided down at a steep angle by the control wire, the chair stopping at the instant one's feet touched bottom. Shrouded figures reached out from the rubble of gleaming wet boulders, the chains were released and the prisoner escorted away from the spray to the gathering gloom. The chair rose again to the surface, and in the shadows men waited for the return. It was a strange dark world, yet in those depths was some ethereal quality of which we were well aware; from the Gothic span, a shaft of light played full upon a group of choirboys.

With eyes upturned to the vaulted roof we watched a minute spider drop on a slender thread, and in the short span of this descent, transform to human shape. By such miracle of vision we could gauge our depth. The guiding cable soared upwards through the shaft, escaping by a hole no bigger than a penny at arm's length, and spanned by a pin. In reality, the hole was the mouth of the chasm, some thirty feet across, and the apparent pin was the approach bridge to the chair.

After all too brief a span for exploration, we were each in turn hoisted to the surface, ready for the hot soup which had been prepared. During the last few feet of the ascent it was expedient to sit back in the chair and walk up the rock to prevent chafing against the sides.

From Gaping Gill, a rough moorland climb brought us to the broad shoulder below the main summit of Ingleborough and a track which skirts the rim provided an easy way to the top. We did not linger; the mist was down, and with it, a heavy drizzle that impelled us to stride out to the far side. The summit commands views that are worthy of the climb, and a plaque erected to commemorate the Coronation of Queen Elizabeth II indicates the directions and distances of surrounding peaks. Penyghent and Whernside are the splendid partners and, together with the distant Lakeland hills, form a contrast to the flats and gleaming sea which lie to the west at Morecambe.

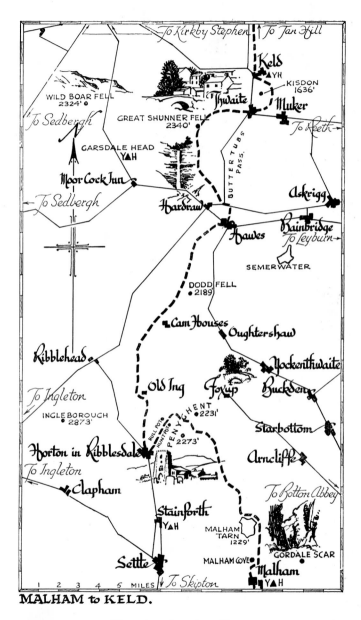

To Kirkby Stephen   To Tan Hill

Keld
YH
KISDON
1636'
Thwaite   Muker
WILD BOAR FELL
2324'
To Sedbergh
GREAT SHUNNER FELL
2340'
To Reeth
GARSDALE HEAD
YH
BUTTER TUBS PASS.
Moor Cock Inn
Askrigg
To Sedbergh
Hardraw
Bainbridge
Hawes
To Leyburn
SEMERWATER
DODD FELL
2189'
Cam Houses   Oughtershaw
Ribblehead
Yockenthwaite
Old Ing   Foxup   Buckden
To Ingleton
INGLEBOROUGH
2873'
PEN Y GHENT
2231'
Starbottom
HULL POT
HUNT POT
2273'
Horton in Ribblesdale
Arncliffe
To Ingleton
Clapham
To Bolton Abbey
Stainforth
YH
MALHAM
TARN
1229'
GORDALE SCAR
MALHAM COVE
Settle   To Skipton
Malham
YH

1 2 3 4 5 MILES

MALHAM to KELD.

There is a hostel at Hawes.

33

Top: Information centre and camp site, Edale. Centre: Fieldhead camp-site, Edale. Bottom: Grindsbrook, first stretch of the Pennine Way.
(Photos: Kenneth Oldham.)

Start of the Pennine Way, Edale, Derbyshire. (Kenneth Oldham.)

On the limestone "clints" at the head of Malham Cove. There are Iron Age field boundaries in a distant field. (Harry Stopford.)

Penyghent, the mountain which dominates the scenery in North Ribblesdale. (Harry Stopford.)

Tan Hill Inn, the highest licensed premises in England. The inn is on the Pennine Way and just inside the Dales National Park.

Although not the highest of the three (Whernside 2,419 ft.), Ingleborough has long claimed the dominant role. It is a traditional "Hill of Fire", enhanced by beacons which have signalled great occasions and crowned with an Iron Age Fort, albeit just a ring of shattered stones. These remnants, hewn from the hillside and laid by distant hands, outline a stronghold of Brigantine tribes, with defensive wall and scattered huts: fragments of a bygone age ravaged by Time and Man. Here was building stone for the beacon and for the Hospice Tower, the short-lived shelter which was raised for shepherds and others who might be caught on the stormy summit. The tower, built under the auspices of Hornby Roughsedge, was opened with such revelry in 1893 that an argument broke forth and it was torn down by drunken vandals. A tumbled heap of stones remains on the summit edge, a silent reminder of the folly of Man. Another thwarted project was the proposed tramway over the summit. This was abandoned in 1898 by force of public opinion before any construction took place. Thus Ingleborough remains, wild and remote, claiming respect from all who toil up her slopes.

In recent years, a more challenging note has been sounded by a "Three Peaks Race". It grew out of a walk which required the contestants to reach the summits of Penyghent 2,273 ft., Ingleborough 2,373 ft. and Whernside 2,419 ft., within a day without using any kind of mechanical assistance. The distance is over 20 miles back to the starting point and involves over 9,000 ft. of ascent and descent. Times vary on this arduous circuit from the walker's eight hours or more to the race record of less than three hours.

However, these are diversionary thoughts which will no doubt come to mind as you stride away from the "Three Peaks" along the Pennine Way route by the west side of Dodd Fell. The great gulf below on your left is the main attraction of this span, after which the "Way" leads steadily downwards into Wensleydale at Hawes.

A flock of unfamiliar sheep is herded past us in the lane, and our query as to breed may bring the sharp reply: "Why, Wensleydale, of course!"

A flagged path by the church confirms our entry into Hawes, a compact market town of solid gritstone houses built so close that roads must zig-zag in between. As a centre of the Wensleydale cheese industry, it holds the advantage of its position astride the dale. The Sedbergh-Northallerton road runs through its axis while Swaledale and Wharfedale are connected through its hub, and Ingleton can be reached by Widdale. The old rail link has gone, but the broad, expansive dale still supports a road down either side while the Ure meanders in between. The great plain is a legacy from glacial times when this was the bottom of a lake.

To the rambler, it is a place to stay or to have a meal. An abundance of guest houses and hotels and the new Youth Hostel more than adequately provide for the needs of the Pennine wayfarer. A good campsite is to be found at Brown Moor Farm, adjacent to the bridge over the Ure.

This will be found to be a relatively easy day, and for those who can ill spare 16 days for the complete traverse of the Pennine Way, there is every good reason to complete the next stage on the same day.

Day 7: Hawes to Keld

O.S. 1:50 000 Map Series Sheets 98 and 91.
12 miles   **Total 110 miles.**
Long climb over moderate ground—walking speed 2½ m.p.h.

Our way leads across the Ure Bridge and clearly signposted pastures to the road by the *Green Dragon Inn* at Hardraw, beyond which the tributary streams from Shunner Fell plunge from a cliff into the confines of a gorge below. This massive limestone shelf looms from the rocky wall and from its lip the fall projects in one great plunge, a hundred feet, and in one splash of seething white it is absorbed into the blackness of its pool. Behind the pool and fall, a tiny track traverses shales beneath the giant overhang and gives the thrilling satisfaction backstage of a thunderous force which rakes us all with spray. Coming from below, it is a variation of our usual encounters with the showers.

In the crescent arc below the fall, a relic bandstand recalls the music of the great brass bands which vied against each other in the contests of the age. This natural amphitheatre has acoustic claims which were refreshed in 1959 when the scene was revived for a B.B.C. recording. Since that time the brass band contests have become an annual event, usually on the first Sunday in May, and the bandstand is to be restored to something of its former glory for the centenary in 1980. To reach Hardraw Force, with its wooded glade, the lawn and Victorian bandstand, we pass through the premises of the Green Dragon Inn and pay a small charge for the privilege. In passing, cast an eye towards the internal decor for this alone will well repay a visit. Many African trophies collected by Mr. Shay enhance the walls, and the inn justly merits a call for refreshment or overnight stay.

On leaving Hardraw the climb of Great Shunner Fell begins and I remember a day when a brilliant sun revealed the splendour of this soaring skyline enhanced by billowing clouds. Among them reared the radiant crowns of crystal ice, giant anvil heads of nimbus form whose shoulders draped dark veils of thunderous rain. We were spared, and continued over Shunner Fell in the warmth and splendour of a summer day.

Ahead lay the summit cairn. At least that's what we thought as we climbed, but there was another beyond, and still more to come. It was one of those prolonged and deceptive approaches, but the route was easy and pleasant underfoot and we reached the summit without feeling that any great effort had been made.

From the north-east tip of Great Shunner Fell an old track drops away towards Swaledale. The old coal pits on the southern flank of Shunner are here replaced by derelict remains of the lead mines. Some of the mines in the area date back to the reign of Henry VIII and a few more distant ones probably originated during the Roman occupation. All of them ceased to be economical and died at the end of the last century.

Thwaite, with its picturesque cottages, nestles below, and beyond rear the Kisdon Heights. The hamlet was the birthplace of the Kearton brothers, renowned naturalists. Richard Kearton, a yeoman farmer, as his father before him, produced numerous books on birds, many of them illustrated, while his brother Cherry was the pioneer of animal photography, including the first film of big game. His film close-ups of wild life, taken without the aid of the long focus lens, are still highly valued among the classic natural history films. A mile away at Muker, inscribed tablets to each of the brothers have been placed on the walls of the village school where they were educated.

You might enjoy a farmhouse tea or even overnight accommodation before taking the footpath which climbs steeply upwards before contouring the eastern side of Kisdon. The hillside drops steeply into Swaledale on the right, and half a mile below Keld, the river plunges over Kisdon Force. A second fall, Catrake Force, on the outskirts of the village is equally splendid, but in contrast to the impacting force of the plunge at Kisdon, Catrake is a broad tumbling fall of pleasing proportions. Almost alongside, the track climbs to the rectangular pattern of houses that form Keld, past the Post Office Store and to the splendid Youth Hostel, a former shooting lodge, dominant on the near skyline as you ascend the hill. Campsites are available at the farm behind the Post Office, but camp high in the midge season. Those torments haunt the trees and lower river pastures. Apart from their attentions, the exploration of the river with its multitude of natural swimming pools, has much to recommend it.

Day 8: Keld to God's Bridge (Pasture End) or to Bowes

10 miles to Pasture End, God's Bridge high level route.
Total 120 miles.

12 miles to Bowes for accommodation   Total 122 miles.

O.S. 1:50 000 Map Series Sheet 91 (and Sheet 92 for "Bowes Loop").

Easy country. Walking speed 3 m.p.h.

The footpath from Keld drops back to Kisdon Force where a bridge spans the river Swale to give access to the steady climb of Stonesdale Moor. The footpath becomes rather undefined as we approach Low Brown Hill and the name of this hill reflects the dominant colour of its tussock grasses. I never pass this way without recalling my first laborious trail as we squelched across the rain sodden moor, forging steadily through mist and rain disturbed by nothing else save the startled owl that suddenly flew out from our feet. Vague figures faded on compass course ahead until the grey shadow of the *Tan Hill Inn*, the highest in England, loomed before us and we sought respite, and while we sipped and chatted around the warm glow of a huge fireside, the storm abated. We signed the visitors' book as the first school party to walk the Pennine Way from Derbyshire to Scotland, bade farewell to our host, and headed off through the last squalls of a storm.

The 1,732 ft. high *Tan Hill Inn* is more than remote. In severe winters it is almost inaccessible. After the snows of 1947, landlord Harry Earnshaw is reputed to have wished "a Happy New Year" to a shepherd who called for a drink in April — the first visitor that year. Michael Parkin relates that a farmer who called during a howling blizzard is said to have asked for "only a half of bitter as I've got the wife waiting outside."

"Bring the poor lass inside for a drink before she freezes to death," urged the astounded landlord.

"Can't do that," said the farmer, downing his drink. "She's died and I'm tekkin' her to the undertaker on me sledge."

We should have been thankful that we only had rain to contend with and, as the storm cleared, we could look out across the shallow

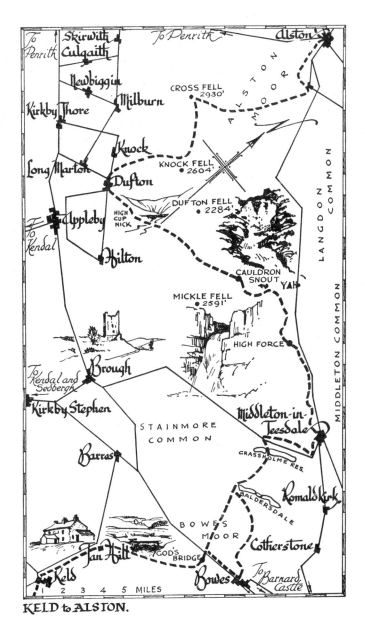

KELD to ALSTON.

There are hostels at Barnard Castle, Dufton and Alston.

41

moorland shelving smoothly from Mickle Fell, the highest Yorkshire peak. Great shafts of sunlight fanned out from the breaking clouds and the distant heather glowed a rich purple. Only one ponderous thunderhead blackened the sky. Raindrops scattered from the heather as we strode across the peaty turf and at the first glimmer of sunshine, the bees returned to their task of collecting dues.

Several tributaries require leaping or fording as the route follows the course of Frumming Beck. A few cairns dot the "Way" which shortly joins an easy track through Sleightholme, a pastoral setting amid the distant purple hues. Sleightholme Beck's turbulent waters pass through a shallow trench-like cleft before we cross by a bridge and just less than a mile ahead reach the parting of the ways. At Trough Heads, the Bowes Loop continues along Sleightholme Beck by East Mellwaters and Lady Mires, whereas the more direct route of the Pennine Way leads north-west to God's Bridge, a natural limestone arch which spans the River Greta. Beyond this, the climb up the A66 Bowes road crosses the site of what was at one time the highest stretch of railway line in England. The old Darlington to Kirkby Stephen line crossed the fell at a height of nearly 1,400 ft., a substantial achievement which carried little weight against the swinging axe of Beeching.

Just across the road is Pasture End. This farm and nearby East Mellwaters have provided camping facilities for my various parties and the real welcome offered to these Pennine walkers has been greatly appreciated.

For those who are not camping, an additional 9½ miles will bring them to Middleton-in-Teesdale where there is abundant accommodation (campers, too, might also wish to lengthen this easy day). Alternatively, at Bowes there are many guest houses and places for meals. The long outline of Dotheboys Hall will bring memories of Dickens' *Nicholas Nickleby* as it is reputed to be the school where the many wretched boys suffered at the hands of William Shaw, characterised as the infamous Wackford Squeers. Today it caters in much better fashion and is to be well recommended. Youth Hostellers will no doubt strike eastwards for the splendid hostel at Barnard Castle.

Day 9:

Pasture End to Langdon Beck

O.S. 1:50 000 Map Series Sheet 91.
17 miles.   **Total 137 miles.**
ALTERNATIVE ROUTE: BOWES TO LANGDON BECK.
Additional 1:50 000 Sheet 92 required for "Bowes Loop".
19 miles.   **Total 141 miles.**
**Walking speed 3 m.p.h. to High Force (14/16 miles),
thereafter 2 m.p.h.**

The Bowes loop adds a total of four miles to the direct route of the Pennine Way. It leaves Bowes by an easy path heading north-west to Levy Pool and joining the direct route at the west end of the Blackton (Balderstone) Reservoir.

The direct route from God's Bridge and Pasture End heads over the pleasant turfy moor to Deepdale Beck where a white footbridge spans the stream. Beyond it, a shallow climb leads over to picturesque Clove Lodge by the three Balderstone Reservoirs. The most recently constructed Balderhead Reservoir has been beautifully landscaped into the surrounding fells and over the following ridge, further reservoirs stretch across the route through Lunedale. A final ridge gives access to the Tees, joining the road alongside the abandoned railway station from which the track has been removed. Over the bridge lies Middleton-in-Teesdale in County Durham, with all the prospects of renewing supplies for the packs or directly catering for the inner man. The major part of this route is now well signposted, although I well remember days when only the map and the Ramblers' Association leaflet could guide; days before some of the route had become a right of way, and Deepdale Beck in particular offered problems which the bridge has solved.

My first confrontation was after days of storm when Deepdale Beck was a torrent reaching waist depth at the point marked on the map as "ford". This was a new, but oft-repeated experience. We had no rope and a human chain might have broken. If you went feet first downstream you might get across, but there were other possibilities! After wandering upstream for half a mile or so, we realised that at all points it was too wide to leap, even at the islands, and the fury of the stream demanded no error of judgment. Young Michael Ogden stood on the brink for some time, water streaming down his sou'wester and yellow cape. His weak smile confirmed that he was ready to end it all! However, we retraced our steps to a flat where the stream widened considerably, and in consequence dissipated its strength over a wide area. Fording was easy at this point, and each boy crossed in turn.

But all of this was nothing to the fury of the Tees. I cannot recall any river in this country with such menacing power as the Tees had on that day. Above the lashing tentacles of spray and general roar and tumult, there could be heard the chilling grinding of boulders along the bottom. High Force, where the Tees plunges 70 ft., was a Niagara. Normally there is just the one fall on the Yorkshire side with a trickle on the Durham bank, and in spate there are twin falls with a monolithic island in between. But on this day, there was just one tumultuous fall which reached the full width of the gorge and covered the island.

The tumult was clearly visible from the road, a quarter of a mile away, but on the approach path the sheeting spray concealed everything but the fury of the force, and a pounding, thunderous roar echoed its own confirmation of the tempestuous scene. It was impossible to go nearer than that.

Serene calm and a crisp early morning light were ours as we looked out from Langdon Beck Youth Hostel on the following day. Hopes were raised, but within the hour, the banners of cirrus came in from the west, and behind these high sweeping curves, a steadily lowering curtain heralded the approach of more rain. Two hours later, the drizzle of a warm front greeted us, and the rain gradually intensified throughout the remainder of the day, only clearing as we descended to Dufton at eight in the evening. However, that was still to come. Our immediate prospect was to view High Force now that the water had to some extent subsided. From the track leading down from the road at the *High Force Hotel* we could see twin falls parted by the rocky bluff.

By a bridge which lies some way downstream, we returned to the Pennine Way on the Yorkshire bank to see High Force from the vantage point which surveyed the island submerged on the previous day. We heard a tale of two men who had been trapped at this spot. They had stepped across to the island with ease from the Durham bank, but during their brief stay, the water rose so quickly that they could not return. One was rescued by rope, but the other was less fortunate.

This rapid rise occurs frequently on the Tees with its large and receptive drainage basin from the slopes of Cross Fell. Although there is peat cover there are large areas where it is of no great depth, and after a period of prolonged rain what peat there is lies sodden, unable to retain the water as a sponge. Under these conditions the run-off is very rapid, and streams and rivers rise suddenly in consequence. During filming operations along this section of the Tees both Ken Holgate and I have recorded a river rise of several feet within the short span of an hour's filming. This is by no means a rare occurrence.

As you peer over the brink of the fall, fascinated by the vaulting waves which arch and spray before the final plunge, you will be conscious of the glistening, black columns of rock which contain the fury within their walls. The rock is dolerite, an igneous material intruded between the carboniferous layers in the distant past. The slow cooling produced crystals of larger size — a coarse-grained rock, but where the rock was chilled in contact with adjacent layers, solidification was more rapid, and the rock has the fine-grained texture of a basalt. This is part of the Whin Sill. It is exposed in the rock face at High Force, and we shall meet it again at Falcon Clints, Caldron Snout, High Cup Nick, and finally as the great ridge along which lies Hadrian's Wall. In places where it has baked the adjacent layers of limestone, a crystalline marble has been formed, and at certain spots this has eroded and is referred to by the descriptive name of sugar limestone.

Above High Force we head north by Cronkley to a bridge across the Tees. This leads directly to the Youth Hostel at Langdon Beck. The original wooden hostel which was burned down has now been replaced by a truly magnificent hostel of stone in contemporary design. It has become a highlight for Pennine travellers. The neighbouring farm, Hill End, offers camping accommodation.

Campers may prefer the wild and remote area near Caldron Snout and they will proceed along the Durham bank where the Pennine Way scrambles among tumbled slabs of rock, an awkward but enjoyable route below the towers of Falcon Clints.

The confluence of the Tees and Maize Beck marks the boundary between three old counties — Yorkshire, Westmorland and Durham. Here the Tees falls 200 ft. in 150 yards at Caldron Snout. This is always spectacular, but in spate, Caldron Snout bursts forth, a boiling, seething mass, disgorging spray to the turbulence downstream. How aptly named these places are: High Force, Falcon Clints, Caldron Snout.

Do not think that the Tees is always in such tempestuous mood. There are times when it is a scene of sheer tranquillity, offering not only the beauty of its scenery and the varied nature of its rocks, but an exciting array within its flora. Rare plants, including the gentian, may still be found in parts of Teesdale. See them, but let them stay that we might enjoy them another day. It is to be hoped that the new Cow Green Reservoir will not destroy the whole of this rare site, or indeed, remove all chances of the spates which so enrich the Teesdale scene that one could almost wish to pass this way in storm. In truth, I have seen the dam preserve the beauty of Caldron Snout on several occasions when Maize Beck has been a dry litter and the waterfall has given sparkle and life to a period of drought.

I have wandered along these banks from Middleton-in-Teesdale, enthralled by the smooth, swirling waters, engulfed here and there by rapids and falls. Low Force, a few miles above Middleton, can be viewed from the suspension bridge across the gorge, and between this fall and the next, High Force, are the pools of deep, clear water.

It is a joy to strip off on the bank and plunge from the heat and toil of the day into such a stream. Every true rambler knows the joys of secret pools and shares them only with a favoured few. In times of drought, a walker is able to enjoy a splash at Caldron Snout, diving into the pool at its base from one of its rocky ledges, and from its cool embrace, emerge, his body no longer tired and pained.

As you climb the rocky staircase to the head of the falls, the great barrier of the Cow Green dam suddenly rears across the skyline, and by the time the ascent is made, it dominates the whole scene. An area which until recently was the most remote in the Pennines now has a surfaced road. The Pennine Way here crosses the bridge which gives access to old Westmorland and the two farm-steads of Birkdale, the noted outposts of human habitation which for long were only accessible on foot or on horseback.

Day 10: Langdon Beck to Dufton

O.S. 1:50 000 Map Series Sheet 91.
15 miles   **Total 152 miles.**
Rough from Falcon Clints to the Maize Beck ford (footbridge), otherwise fairly easy ground. Walking speed: 2½ m.p.h.

From Caldron Snout the 4½ miles to High Cup Nick climb steadily and are well cairned, even to the point where best to ford Maize Beck. Through mist and rain progress will be entirely guided by compass and the cairns are a pleasant reassurance of the track. Fording Maize Beck can be a major task when the stream is in spate. Although no more than 12 ft. across it can on occasions reach well up to the thighs (the new footbridge upstream can be used).

High Cup Nick offers a startling panorama of crag scenery. Approaching from Maize Beck it appears as a great scoop taken from the face of the Pennines. You can perch on the edge, and on either hand the great precipitous arc sweeps round, a giant horseshoe etched on the sides of the hills. These cliffs are again the bastions of the great Whin Sill, the blue-grey dolerite which adds splendour to many a Pennine scene. Here, great buttresses with jagged whinstone tops support and lend stark thrill to a mountain scene. The walls drop sheer, and frost-shattered rock fans out below to give the scale. All this lies below 2,000 ft.

Dufton Post Office has provided refuge for many of my parties, is no doubt that the stretch from High Force and Caldron Snout, terminating by way of High Cup Nick at Dufton, offers one of the wildest and most stimulating sections of the Pennine Way.

Dufton's charm is enhanced by the warmth and colour of its walls and houses, the rosy tints of Eden's sandstone, and by their rectangular pattern around the green. This arrangement, as the suffix of its name, betrays a Saxon origin. Its spacious form and avenue of trees lend tranquillity to a scene which may at any time be shattered by the full vent of the Helm Wind, a phenomenon which swoops down with such force that hay ricks may be stripped and huts overturned.

Small wonder that the residents smile and drop a hint of warning when campers pitch their tents in the vicinity. The onslaught of the Helm would be an uplifting experience in more ways than one. I have always been spared, but my visits tend to be in summer. It is in winter and spring that the Helm has its full lease, although it is not unknown at other seasons. It sweeps down in spring, transforming the landscape overnight as new, green shoots lie blanched and desiccated to a deathly pallor.

When a cold north-easterly wind crosses the Pennines, it descends the steep western slopes and comes into contact with the relatively warm air of the Eden Valley. This naturally rises and the potential vacuum is filled by a steadily increasing onrush of cold air from across the Pennines. The force of the wind is thus concentrated in a downrush from the western slopes and expends itself within the limited range of the Eden or occasionally beyond. The rising air cools and a condensation layer forms along the edge of the fells (the Helm) and a second cloud, a slender, rolling pencil shaft grows rapidly to form the Bar or Burr which is said "never to cross the River Eden; nor does the strength of wind". The Bar does, in fact, mark the limit of the wind.

The colour of the Helm is often a forecast of events: the Black Helm will be accompanied by rain, but the White Helm is the harsh desiccating wind of the winter months which may blow for several days or even weeks. "If it blows for a week, it will blow for three", is a local saying which bears a good deal of truth and many tales may be heard of hurtling slates or chimney-pots, of fallen trees and men prostrate before a force, pitting themselves against its fury, only to crawl away from its unyielding strength.

Yet on such days, in some parts of Eden, one could walk with a lighted candle and scarcely a breeze may be felt in Birkdale. Coming from Birkdale, you can see the cloud and hear the roar, and when you step into it, buttons will fly if it is up to full strength. It has been said that goose "nebs" (beaks) have blown off and one of the farmers claims to having one of his father's huge Angus bulls blown onto an outbuilding roof — a slight exaggeration, no doubt! These stories, passed on to me by Mr. Lightburn, are a vivid portrayal of how the strength of the Helm was explained a few decades ago. He also offered another version of the saying. "If it blows for three days it will blow for nine, and if it blows for nine, it will blow for twelve weeks." Although Mr. Lightburn has known the wind to stay off and on for some considerable time, he has never witnessed more than a continuous week. Campsites and other accommodation, including a new Youth Hostel replacing Knock, may be found at Dufton.

Day 11: Dufton to Alston

O.S. 1:50 000 Map Series Sheets 91 and 86.
22 miles.   **Total 174 miles.**
Very strenuous day—walking speed 2 m.p.h.

The conical hills, Murton Pike, Dufton Pike and Knock Pike, which rise abruptly at the base of the fells, consist of pre-Carboniferous Skiddaw Slates and Borrowdale Volcanics and are known as the Crossfell Inlier (a miniature exposure of Lake District type rocks). They form vivid contrast to the reds of Eden's sandstones or the great dark wall of the Pennines which rises abruptly behind with a massive displacement of the Carboniferous rocks (some 7,000 ft.) along the line of the Pennine Fault.

A small track to the north end of Dufton runs between Dufton and Knock Pike and closes alongside Great Rundale Beck for a short distance before the foot bridge. This is the start of the long toil to the summit of Cross Fell, the highest peak of the Pennines (2,930 ft.).

After crossing Rundale Beck the track heads toward Swindale Beck, but on the approach, swerves to due east and cuts up to High Scald Fell. At this turning, the Pennine Way follows its more northerly route to cross Swindale and then climbs to the summits of Green and Knock Fell. The climb is moderately steep but the ground is good—short fescue and shallow peat—and the going is pleasant exercise.

Excavations and spoil heaps, the evidence of mining days, are bypassed on the approach to Great Dun Fell. Green Castle lies just below as we plod across the expansive dome of the fell, crossing the road to the Radio Station a couple of times to avoid the large "S" bend (and, indeed, the road walking, too). In this way, and by skirting a further shale trench, the Radio Station, that unmistakable landmark of the summit, is reached. I confess that I have never seen the sun shining on this plot of land, for on each occasion of my journeying this way, the clouds have only just cleared the summit or else formed a shroud of swirling mist from which the massive towers loomed suddenly ahead.

For smooth contours and curves, it is hard to beat the sequence of Great Dun Fell and Little Dun Fell, culminating on Cross Fell. Little Dun Fell is the nearest to a pinnacle dome, but its more gently rounded neighbours have each the advantage of height. Between them, the hillsides sweep down to a morass of spongy turf and bog, the south-east flank of Cross Fell being the source of the River Tees. Even in times of drought it is a wet crossing, but in contrast, the shoulders and summits of these hills are dry and firm, with only a shallow covering of peat and turf. Cross Fell is littered with the fragmented rock befitting the topmost Pennine Peak, and the summit is crowned with both cairn and trig. point.

The smooth, dominant outline of Cross Fell sweeps down to Eden unbroken by the crags and sharp edges which characterise so many Pennine heights. It excels more by its massive proportions and the view from the summit, a view which reaches beyond the vale to the silvery Lakes in a setting of distant grandeur. Some little time may be spent identifying the blue-grey outlines of familiar Lakeland hills. Ullswater reaches out from Helvellyn, and to the north, the bold metallic sheen of the Solway cuts deeply into the dark land mass. Beyond it lies Scotland.

This enchanting view, the ever changing atmosphere of cloud and storm, of shafts of sun on distant peaks or glimmering on some strip of shore; the golden lake and radiant sunset strands — all these and more are offered at your door should tents be pitched the night on Cross Fell's summit. And if the wind restrains from veering to a Helm, you might observe the dawn! There is, too, that other possibility — that Cross Fell will remain vague and grey, a plateau top of shattered grit with cairn and obelisk at the summit and a compass pointing to the misty north. Should you turn too much to the north, descent will be over rough and tumbled scree, but the Pennine Way makes the easy north-west slopes to join an old mine track on its easterly course.

This track, connecting Kirkland with Garrigill on the South Tyne, makes a pleasant change from untrodden moor and, with a good pace, we may skirt the extensive drainage basin of Black Burn. At Kirkland in Eden, the mine track follows the line of Maiden Way, but the routes part before the climb. Maiden Way skirts with unheeding straight line the western side of Green Fell, Black Burn and the South Tyne, whereas the mine track follows the contours to the east by Skirwith Fell and thence to the north by Long Man Hill.

The old track was once a funeral trail whence the sad bereaved of Garrigill would heave their precious burden to be interred in consecrated ground, as were their ancestors, at Kirkland. After one procession had been halted by the snow and the corpse had lain for two weeks on the moor, a corner of Garrigill was consecrated so that the trail was used no more by coffin bearers.

Old mine workings dot the area and along the track may be found the fragments of their spoils. Among the pickings you will find blue fluorspar, the Blue John which is generally believed to be found only in the Winnats, near Castleton in Derbyshire. Let them lie that others might share the pleasure.

Do not underestimate this way from Dufton. It is a good trek, and the day will be long if you care to spend some time on the summit. The sharp plunge of our route into Garrigill on the South Tyne is enhanced by the prospect of food. The *George and Dragon* provides good fare at a moderate price, a welcome respite which might induce you to linger.

From the sombre colours of the gritstone moors, the luxuriant green of the South Tyne appears as a haven, with the river a source of matchless pleasure. Garrigill would delight any angler who cares to snatch a fly across the water, and the ramble along the South Tyne affords the splendour of river scenery with lush pastures and woodlands on the banks, occasional deep pools and a clarity of water that beckons one to plunge.

Climbing some little way above the river, we follow the topmost edge of the woodland fringe, and below us, the absorbing pattern of sunlit leaves and sparkling water follows our course along the eastern bank to Alston, the highest market town in England.

It is hard to believe that most of Alston lies at 1,000 ft. or more above sea level. The surrounding fields are rich with the green or gold of pasture and arable, but the contrast of the valley with the surrounding higher moors and the steep cobbled road through the centre emphasises the close margin between the two.

The sad loss by demolition of the old Youth Hostel by the cobbled square has at last been redeemed by the opening of a new hostel of superior grade directly on the Pennine Way as it enters Alston from the south. Alston is a valuable centre for supplies as the proud title, "highest market town in England", suggests, but to be truthful it can scarcely retain its title since it only holds two markets—in May and October. It nevertheless possesses great tourist attraction with a particularly strong pull towards Tyneside.

The church of Alston is dedicated to St. Augustine, who by legend dispelled the demons of the storms which had their homes on Fiends Fell. This being done, a cross was erected on the highest summit which bears the name to this day—Cross Fell. Thus is Alston connected to and isolated by this great massif.

Terraces of houses rise up cobbled streets, high and steep; open shops and flagstone pavements; gables, lintels and stone steps thrusting to the fore, or gritstone stairs as access to some second storey door—the spice of unconformity. And by the shelter in the square, you sit and look across the cobbled Market Place.

Alston has great character and there is no lack of hotels or guest houses to cater for the walker. Campers will find a campsite between the station and the river.

Day 12: Alston to Hadrian's Wall

O.S. 1:50 000 Map Series Sheet 86.
22 miles.   **Total 196 miles.**
Very strenuous day. Easy to moderate footpath routes to Greenhead. Strenuous on the Wall. Estimated walking speed 3 m.p.h. for the first fifteen miles to Greenhead and 2 m.p.h. for the remaining seven along the Wall to Twice Brewed. New Youth Hostel at Greenhead.

Immediately across the Tyne Bridge at Alston, the Pennine Way strikes northwards along the banks of the Tyne to Harbut Lodge before heading west by the north flank of Park Fell to join the Maiden Way in its western circuit of the Roman Fort, Whitley Castle. Returning once again to river pastures, our way meanders between road and rail, hugging the verdant strip between the fells. This is no monotonous moorland trek, but the gradual unfolding of a tale. Each day has new and varied scenes; each day, a challenge or a thrill. Now we slip back into the past and take the Maiden Way.

Climbing from Burnstones the Roman Road appears more clearly on the ground and by the Glendue Burn as a pencil line is etched on the far hillside, a lighter patch between the green of an arable plot and the darker bracken against the wall. Here is the contrast with the modern road which contours round to cut up the burn with a stiff elbow bend. Some miles ahead the skyline rears to a line of crags, the northern outcrop of the Great Whin Sill. Along this line lies Hadrian's Wall.

The heath and heather track gives way to the harsh landscape of a colliery, but this, too, slides away, engulfed by the rich green pastures of the Hartley Burn. The green pales to fawn as we cross by the north side of Hartleyburn Common, but all eyes now are fixed ahead — to the line of crags across from Greenhead. We know at last we have reached the Wall.

To stand upon the ramparts of the Great Whin Sill and on the Wall itself is to become absorbed in the history of a nation, for this line, stretching seventy-three miles from the Solway to the mouth of the Tyne, marks the northern limit of the Roman Empire. This was decided by Emperor Hadrian when he came to Britain in A.D. 121 to survey the frontier land. Here lies the firm defensive line he eyed, with the graceful waves of the Great Whin Sill sweeping up from the south in gentle line to end abruptly, poised to the north, as breakers petrified.

Here was to be established a permanent frontier, a continuous rampart ten feet thick, built of stone and filled with rubble, rising with the parapet to 20 ft. high on its northern side. It was to be protected on the north by a 30 ft. ditch and strengthened by the mobility of its troops along a military way to the south. Garrisons were to be housed in 16 forts along the line, with mile castles and turrets in between. All these things we shall see as we make our way by Thirlwall Castle and the track by Walltown to the Nine Nicks of Thirlwall at the start of a strenuous tour. To be correct, there are only seven "nicks" since quarrying has removed two, and the Wall with them. In fact if blasting is not indicated by the warnings, we might peer over the edge of Greenhead Quarry to see how it has eaten into the rock and the remnants of the Wall. It would be wrong to claim that the quarry had destroyed the Wall, for as we pursue our course you will find only a remnant of the former glory, a skeleton trail that winds from crag to crag and almost up the vertical sides. The Thirlwall Castle ruins betray the fate of stones that once were laid at Rome's command. Pillaged and plundered to its very bones, these remnants of the Wall still mark the boundary of this Roman stand.

A turret and mile castle can be traced across the summits of the "Nicks", and beyond, the fort of Aesica stands in passive quiet on its grassy ledge. The ramparts are still visible, though much overgrown, and on the west rise to seven or eight courses with an unusual bonding course of wafer stones. Traces of the Guard Room and Barracks may be found, but all is ruin, and heaps of turf and stone embroidered with waving grass and harebells mark out the rest. The north-east corner is obliterated by a farm.

A little to the east the ochreous scar of extensive quarrying marks another region of desolation where the further destruction of a good section of the Wall has made this a heavy price to pay for whinstone. Almost on the verge are the foundations of Cawfields Mile Castle which can be seen in plan as we approach.

To the south and on a parallel course to the Wall, the Vallum cuts across the marshy common and we traverse a section of this ditch to learn the nature of its plan and to consider, too, its purpose, for this is still disputed. The great ditch, broad and flat bottomed with the upcast mounds of earth as ramps some twenty feet from either side, has been filled across in places to give access from the Military Road to the Wall and beyond. This might confirm that it was not part of the defensive system quite apart from its position south of the Wall. More recent opinion ventures the possibility of its being connected with customs dues, and as this responsibility was a civil affair, it is not unreasonable to suppose that it was kept apart from the military — and the Wall.

High Force, Teesdale, on the old border between Yorkshire and County Durham. When the river has risen quickly, people have been trapped on the rock island between the two torrents. (Harry Stopford.)

Like a prophet crying in the wilderness, Caldron Snout thunders in isolation. (Harry Stopford.)

Alston, the Cumbrian market town near the 1,000 feet contour, claims to be the highest market town in England. (Harry Stopford.)

Hadrian's Wall in its most spectacular stretch. (G. N. Wright.)

The new youth hostel and National Park Information Centre at Byrness.
(Kenneth Oldham.)

Left:
The youth hostel
at Kirk Yetholm
can sleep 30
people. To the
left of the
photograph is the
old packhorse
bridge.
(David Joy.)

ALSTON to BELLINGHAM.

Youth Hostels have now been opened at Alston and Greenhead.

It is here that the Wall climbs to its highest point, the summit of Whinshields Crag, 1,230 ft. above sea level. To the south, the sweeping lines of hills grow from the distant pale grey outline of Cross Fell. Behind us now lie the whole of the Pennines, and more to the west a few reared heads mark Lakeland still, but to the north this broad sweeping landscape acclaims a distant line of hills: of pale tints of purple and rosy sheen. We have come at last to face the Cheviot Hills.

On Whinshields Crag, an eight foot wall stands on a platform ten feet wide. The extra width projects as a lip on the southern side, while to the north is the smooth defensive face. The apparent unconformity grew from a change of plan. When work on the Wall was already well advanced, economy decided that it should be eight feet wide instead of ten. However, a great part west of Newcastle had already been constructed at the former width together with the forts and mile castles which were to hang as pendants from the Wall. Elsewhere, the foundations had been laid and this explains the appearance of a narrow wall on a broader ledge.

The Wall was built in sections, each some 35 to 40 yards in length under the direct command of a Centurion, and it is not surprising that the joints between them did not always conform. These poor joints, or "offsets", are another source of human interest which the Wall displays. Remember, too, that the Wall was reconstructed two or three times in places after the violent onslaughts from the north, and that each reconstruction made some variance. What we see is more of the work of the Third Century than of Hadrian's time.

A minor road cuts across our track and heads south to cross the Greenhead road where the latter follows the course of the Vallum. At this crossing, the *Twice Brewed Inn* and the Once Brewed Youth Hostel each in their own way cater for the needs of the Pennine Way travellers as well as the hosts who come to see the Wall. My camping parties have always made polite requests at one or other of the various farms along this stretch and have invariably been made to feel very welcome. When we leave, not a trace of our stay is visible on the ground and we leave our kind hosts in no doubt about our appreciation of their hospitality. This is the least return, for the goodwill of the farmers is something that every country lover must value most highly.

Day 13: Once Brewed Hostel (Hadrian's Wall) to Bellingham

O.S. 1:50 000 Map Series Sheets 86 and 80.
14 miles.   **Total 210 miles.**
Moderately strenuous day. Walking speed 2½ m.p.h.

Once Brewed Youth Hostel was entirely rebuilt in 1968 and now includes an information centre for the Northumberland National Park as well as a large car park and associated amenities. A model of the Wall with much information and recorded explanations makes a visit to the centre well worthwhile.

South of the inn and the Once Brewed Hostel, the Roman Stanegate pursues its steady course, but the Pennine Way returns to the Whin Sill. Away to the east, the scattered remnants of the Wall rise to a firm enduring line which twists and turns from crag to crag: great sinew of the Roman might flexed across the gaps of time.

The Wall sweeps on beyond Peel Crag, across the gulf where shattered remnants mark its stand. No sooner down than it is up again by some precipitous way which scales the tops. But this is not for long, for other inroads cut into this hump backed route. A further steep descent is made to Castle Nick where we see exposed the seven course walls of Milecastle 39 with a massive gateway, broader than most, but made of smaller stones. There would be difficulty in transporting large ones to this wild spot. These mile castles are placed at intervals of Roman miles along the Wall, a Roman mile being equivalent to some 1,650 yards, and between each pair of castles may be found the remains of two turrets, the signalling towers which helped to maintain contact along the line.

Another steep ascent is made, and then a further rift, Steep Gap, where the Wall is built with stones which lie in horizontal plane instead of parallel to the ground. This gives a step formation to the steep incline, a jagged edge which adds a rugged splendour to the rocks we climb, reaching now the crag above the lough, the steep precipitous face which rises from the screes below. These same basaltic columns we have seen before are here displayed with grandeur unsurpassed, bedecked with ferns and waving grass and crowned with purple heather tussocks.

From our vantage point above Crag Lough, we see the rolling waves of wind stir through the reeds beside the mere, combing smooth their waving strands then sweeping out across the water with the streaking lines of foam to mark its track. The trees above the crag are swaying in the breeze with branches clawing wildly in the live interpretation of a dance, and through this silhouetted screen of waving branches, we look towards the emerald green of Hotbank Crags. The deep shadow of a cloud moves swiftly over, and for a while the world is dark and sullen, then the radiant glow spreads out across the landscape as the cloud moves on, and all is riches once again. Descending now between the trees, we make our way to Milking Gap where a grass plateau near Hotbank Farm marks the outline of another castle.

Look back from here across the vast extent of the line of crags, and see these giant breakers rolling up from the south, a rampant screen of purplish hue, poised to the north, with deep black shadows at their base. The jewel waters of Crag Lough remain a vivid blue: deep sapphire set in a mount of jet. This setting may be framed by swaying branches of the rustic pines as we climb the Hotbank Crags; then all is lost behind and we become absorbed in the way ahead.

Below, to the right, the clear line of the Vallum cuts its parallel course, while the Wall sweeps on in its own indomitable way, rising, falling, twisting and turning with such beauty of form that this must be the finest part. It is along here, beyond Rapishaw Gap and following the line of Cuddy's Crags that we reach the most photographed section of Hadrian's Wall as it tilts and rolls across the gulf and up towards the fort of Housesteads. This rhythmic rise and fall along the crests of waves is repeated on the skyline with the form of Sewing-shields Crag. Before we reach the fort we pass the Housesteads Mile Castle (37) excavated to reveal its features, the best of which are displayed in the northern gateway which is in a better state of preservation than any other excavated example. A direct span of Wall along the tree-lined summit of the Crag connects this castle with the fort at Housesteads, one of the best preserved Roman forts in the country. There is a museum at Housesteads, containing some interesting exhibits of the site and a large-scale model of the fort as it once stood. It is worth obtaining the guide book issued by the Ministry of the Environment.

The Pennine Way now doubles back, and for a span of half a mile we walk again the sturdy spine, along a crag bedecked with pine — this firm reminder of the Roman will that nobly strides the wave crests of the Great Whin Sill. And as we tread along these curves, which flex and twist with welded strength and beauty all at hand. we cannot but confirm: it is the finest Roman relic in our land.

North of the Wall lies a countryside of clean, bare hills. Here are expansive tracts with shallow clefts gleaned smooth by ice sheets of another age. Across this land we head towards the shallow loughs, more remnants of our glacial past, and pass between the largest of these lakes.

This lovely setting of the clean swept hills, with sparkling water lapping softly by the shores of loughs, is ours for just a little way — a pleasant interlude of flashing water and forever bobbing birds on

Green Lee Lough in contrast to the passive blue of Broomlee, where cattle stand in silence at the water's edge and nose among the gently swaying reeds.

To the south is the vast expanse of ramparts of the Great Whin Sill, extending out on either side, a massive fortress wall which marks the boundary of the Roman might. Behind us now the loughs and Wall; in front is the ever-changing scene. The clean sweeping hills are here replaced by the verdant cloak of heavy green. Expanding forests of the spruce have overwhelmed this smooth landscape, and now provide a living screen of towering spires, with broad straight gaps, the fire breaks, in between.

Thus we pass through the span of forests and out again to the wind-swept moor with fawns and browns of wiry grasses replacing the forest's needled floor. A trodden path makes an easy way by the tussock heads of the open moor and we pass near the site of Kimmin's Cross, an upright pillar which marks a spot where a chief was slain by the sons of his host for want of gain.

The legend tells how the chief (Cumming) was well received by King Arthur, and on his departure was presented with a golden cup. This so displeased King Arthur's sons that they set out in pursuit and a cross was erected to mark the spot of their foul deed. Legends of King Arthur also connect to Sewingshields Crag where a hidden cave conceals the sleeping forms of King Arthur, Queen Guinevere, the Court of the Round Table, and even the Royal hounds, all under enchantment "until someone shall enter, blow the bugle and cut the garter with a sword of stone". Further legends relate them to the King Crags and Queen Crags near Broomlee.

Another forest track leads on near Willow Bog, a small oasis in the great plantations, then on again through a further woodland break to a point where the path divides, one track leading east by the clean lines of Sadbury Hill, and our way striding north across this smooth and gently rolling countryside.

Two small ridges lie before the North Tyne: an easy grassy rise across Wark Common, and beyond, the pleasant climb of Shitlington Crag, a rocky scarp which leads to heather moor beyond. The many streams which lie across our route are added spice to the pleasure of this way. We might enjoy the northern flavour of their names for, thinking back along our route, we have travelled from the Derbyshire cloughs and Cheshire brooks, by Yorkshire's becks and gills, and now to the Scottish counterpart in a land of sikes and burns.

From the rise at Ealingham Rigg we look across the valley of the North Tyne and make our descent of this shallow heather moor to the outskirts of Bellingham where we join the road near the Brown Rigg Camp School.

This marks the end of another stage in the journey, for here is a Youth Hostel where we might stay, or camp if we will, by the North

Tyne. Bellingham is the last main centre for supplies before we reach the end of the journey 43 miles distant. On my last camping journey this way, we purchased all our supplies at Bellingham except for eggs and milk which we felt sure we could pick up at Byrness. However, the hens were not in lay and all we could muster between the nine of us were three eggs and two pints of milk. Luckily we carried flour and were thus able to toss pancakes on the summits of the Cheviots, an unusual but very satisfying alternative to the scrambled eggs which had been planned for the following morning.

Across the road from the *Fox and Hounds* stands a church with a very fine arched roof of stone, there being only one other like it in the country. Alongside this church is a strange long tomb, the Long Pack, where a nameless brigand is said to be buried. The story was related to me by the late Mrs. Potts of the *Fox and Hounds*, who said that some four miles lower down the Tyne is a very fine mansion, Lee Hall. This was the home of a Colonel Ridley who returned home from India in 1723 and rebuilt it in a very elegant and costly manner. The service of plate alone was said to be valued at a thousand pounds. Annually, during the winter months, the Colonel took his family away to London and left the Hall in the care of his domestics. On this occasion there were only three remaining on duty; the maid, Alice, and two men who threshed the corn and looked after the cattle and outbuildings. Apparently a pedlar came to seek lodgings for the night, and although he flattered and coaxed the maid, he was not allowed to stay. He did, however, persuade her to allow him to leave for the night a very strange and bulky pack which he carried.

During the evening the long package was seen to move and one of the men, a youth in fact, shot the bundle where it lay. On hearing the final cry of anguish and seeing the blood pour from the pack, it was opened to reveal the body of a well-built man. With him, inside the bundle were four loaded pistols, a cutlass and a silver wind call (whistle). It was realised that the whistle was to summon further assailants when the robber had cut himself free and possibly added murder to his score, and so the Colonel's retainers were summoned to help. By nightfall they all lay in hiding armed with pitchforks, old swords and cudgels, waiting for the robbers to appear. At a blast of the whistle a party of horsemen appeared and was ambushed as it entered the grounds. Four of their number were killed, but during the night their bodies were carried away so that none could identify the brigands. The body from the pack was laid for inspection for a fortnight but no-one could recognise him and the Colonel had him buried, nameless, at Bellingham. The shape of the tomb is as a long pack and carved into the stone are the pistols, a cutlass and a whistle.

This countryside of the North Tyne has known full well the trail of thieves and robbers, for it was a route of the Liddesdale raiders who swept down from Scotland, and it had its own crop of brigands, the moss-troopers who roamed all this terrain from their strongholds on the Wall and the peel-houses scattered among these remote and windswept hills. Their records of pillage and plunder were confined chiefly among the poorer folk who could not retaliate as could the richer lord or squire. Oddly enough, it was their stronghold by Housesteads which protected this fine section of the Wall from the same fate that was served elsewhere, and by this strange twist of fate, they have handed down this rich jewel of our heritage.

Day 14:   Bellingham to Byrness
O.S. 1:50 000 Map Series Sheet 80.
15 miles.   **Total 225 miles.**
Moderate ground—walking speed 2½ m.p.h.

From Bellingham we turn to the north, following the track by Blakelaw and Hareshaw House. If time permits make a diversion up the course of Hareshaw Burn, a pretty glen with surfaced track and bridges leading to the face of the Linn where the sides close in and the stream tumbles down for 100 ft. By retracing our steps for some 300 yards from this point we can zig-zag up the steep hillside to continue the Pennine Way along the heights to Abbey Rigg. This is a countryside of burnished grass and purple heather with a few Scots Pines grouped near to Hareshaw House. Across these pastures roam the herds of Galloways, those splendid beasts with glossy tufted coats of black which make a picture in this highland scene. Among them, too, are the Highland cattle with widespread horns and shaggy hair which waves and blows as freely as the grasses on which they contentedly graze.

We cross the road near Abbey Rigg by a little row of miners' cottages and climb again the gentle shelving ridge of Lough Shaw, Deer Play and Lord's Shaw, keeping on the summit crown, an easy way compared with the basin between which offers swamp and more difficult ground. The higher track is of purple heather, a smooth, soft carpet of royal hue, which leads to another road below Lord's Shaw and this to a grassy track reaching out by Gib Shiel. This lonely farmstead is set high among the fells where the fresh cut fields close by and the grazing horse confirm the continued presence of mankind.

The final stage to the river Rede is through forestry plantation. The track is a fire break between the trees, and periodically as we climb a rise, we face the flimsy structure of the fire observation posts. I have seen the swift brown form of a fox pass quickly across

BELLINGHAM to KIRK YETHOLM.

There is a hostel at Byrness, north-west of Rochester.

63

these trackways and on my last journey north we camped at Blakehopeburnhaugh, the longest name on the Pennine Way. If you camp on this site do not overlook a shared attraction which midges have for trees and water. In late summer you will do well to climb to higher ground.

Across the bridge the Pennine Way strikes by the river bank into Byrness. The local garage has a café and those requiring accommodation can choose between the Byrness Hotel or the newly opened Youth Hostel by the green at the far side of the village. The hostel accommodates twenty-two but neither meals nor store are provided, although there is a shop and Post Office nearby. Part of the Youth Hostel building is laid out as an information centre. Make a final check of all provisions for on the morrow you will climb the Cheviot Hills. The final stretch of 27 miles is truly the sting in the tail to be accomplished within the day by all save the camper. It is he who will find the true heart of the Cheviots, settling down within its folds and having time to linger on its fells.

Days 15 and 16: Byrness to Cheviot and Kirk Yetholm

O.S. 1:50 000 Map Series Sheets 80 and 74.
27 miles. **Total 252 miles.**
Very strenuous—walking speed 2 m.p.h.

The Cheviots mark the final chapter of our journey, the last great rise before our goal for here, the rolling, sweeping slopes give way to the thrusting hills which lie astride the border.

A steep climb through the forest break gives access to Byrness Hill and the long grassy ridge which climbs steadily to the north. It is a landscape of smooth, curving hills, arching one upon the other as we climb to Ravens Knowe. This is also a countryside of pale straw grasses, polished and burnished by the wind and sun. Deep in the valleys are occasional farms like Cottonshope with its two or three trees, a tiny patch of green, and the brown and tawny forms of Highland cattle grazing close alongside. Cottonshope Head marks the last outpost with a brave patch of green etching its claim on the pale silvery hillside. Beyond it lies Dere Street, the Roman road which runs along the ridge by Outer Golden Pot, the hollowed stone that lies along the track.

Sheep roam freely across these hills, seeking the good green pasture of some steeper slopes. They are the renowned aristocrats of the sheep world, the Cheviots, descended from an ancient race on these volcanic hills. Legend claims that they swam ashore from the Armada, and very possibly the Elizabethan ruff at the neck has fortified their claim to this great age, but one has only to note the proud Roman nose to realise that they arise from a much more ancient stock than that. They are by expression alone a distinguished race, and their pure white wool remains neat and unblemished — a sure sign of good breeding, and, of course, of a landscape clean as the crystal air.

Ravens Knowe sometimes displays a massive red flag indicating activity on the Army range at Coquet Head, but take no heed. Our route lies clear to the north-west by Ogre Hill, which offers that joyous moment as the horizon dips and the Border lies before you. Here at last is the great climax of our tour as we walk along the Border Fence and take the final plunge to Yetholm.

I remember once planning this journey from the map, scanning the peaks along this great ridge and thinking that once the general height had been reached, the rest would be easy. Do not yourselves be so deceived. This is one of the hardest day's walking in the whole of our journey, for the twenty-seven miles of these high summits are tufted coarse grass and heather, much of which has grown leggy and requires high knee raising for miles on end. An early start is a great advantage in the crossing of this final crest.

The Border Fence is crossed by a gate at the foot of Ogre Hill and from there is followed in its eastward descent of the Coquet Burn to the Roman Camps at Chew Green. The familiar pattern of the square is repeated here as a double figure etched upon the brink of Coquet Head. It is easier to discern its form from the distant slopes than it is when picking your way across the ditches and rampart mounds. Such Roman Camps are dotted through the Cheviot Hills along the line of Dere Street, which connected north from Roman York to Scotland.

But now the "Way" assumes a constant grandeur with steep sided valleys cutting deep on either side and occasional screes of pink granite rock revealing the inner secrets of this vast dome. The whole of the Cheviots is of volcanic origin, for here in the earliest Devonian times stood an active volcano which poured out this great mountain mass. Still further igneous rocks were intruded within the main and these give rise to the large mass of pink granite displayed by the screes in the middle of these uplands. Prolonged and active erosion left nothing but a deeply dissected volcanic base which in turn lay beneath the sheets of ice in glacial times. All this is revealed in the smoothed and rounded surface and the numerous dry valleys which cut across spurs as glacial overflow channels. Much, too, is buried under cover of glacial deposits.

Thus we stride on, the deep green gulfs cutting in on either side of a summit ridge of burnished grass and purple heather. These higher slopes are dry and better drained than on the Pennines further south; they enjoy more sun and form a suitable home for the adder or viper. These venomous snakes like to bask in the sun and it is not unlikely that as you tread your way, a warning hiss will tell you of their presence. I have only walked along this ridge on two occasions, and both times came across the viper. Do not destroy these creatures should you see them. The hiss of danger warns you where to tread, for the adder will glide quietly away into cover if it has the chance.

Broad Flow, Lamb Hill and Beefstand Hill follow close upon each other, this latter peak is a broad and shallow dome of darkened tints of a heather moor, a giant beefsteak, limp and placid, draped across the saddle.

You scramble over this and some distance ahead lie Mozie Law and Windy Gyle, the long continuous chain of peaks that stretches on for mile after mile, and all the time along this route your eyes will rove across the broad expanse of the Scottish scene from the Eildon Hills and the distant Tweed to the Cheviot foothills' lavish tongues of green. This is the route of high knee raising; of tussock grass and furrowed peat with tangled lengthy heather branches clawing wildly at your feet.

To cover the whole twenty-seven miles (twenty-five if you skip Cheviot) in one day is hard going. To cover it in two stages by spending the night on the summit is still hard going, but you have more time to enjoy it!

In the drought of 1959 my party camped by Windy Rigg. All the streams were dry and empty from the source and we had to resort to shallow peaty pools for our supply. Most were only the size of a hand basin and some were green with algae, but a few had crystal water slowly filtering through and from these we skimmed the top few inches into our containers. As we turned in for that last night of our journey, refreshed by a good curry on the cool summit, we witnessed the superb beauty of a Cheviot sunset, the tents silhouetted against a gold, then crimson sky. The smooth dark lines of the Cheviot Hills were on every side thrown up in relief by the icy light of a very full moon. This was the climax to our walk.

A deep red gash against the sky revealed the dawn the following day, and from it spread those golden shafts of early morning light that strike across the hills as heralds of another glorious day. On this camping journey of seventeen days we had experienced only three showers of rain, two of them at night, and the whole of the Pennines suffered from drought in contrast to the deluge and spate which showered upon us for fourteen days out of seventeen in that fateful August of 1952. August is a bad month for the Pennines if you wish to see the sun.

The sweeping grassy ridge leads up to Windy Gyle and we follow the Border Fence around a broad expansive arc to an arrow head which leads to Cairn Hill Summit. From here, a mile of moor with wasting peat and heather gives access to the summit of the Cheviot. The trig. point lies within the plateau summit and to enjoy the distant scene one must needs traverse to the further edge and cross again for the change of view.

The summit itself is one of the least inspiring on our way and if you wish to walk across its airy spaces you will need to retrace your steps a mile to the summit of Cairn Hill. Auchope Cairn, half a mile away, marks the start of the steep descent with the drop to Auchope Rigg. To the right lies Hen Hole, a deep ravine, where the granite is exposed in rocky crags. There are a very few exposures of the rock within these hills.

The Schil is the last big climb on our Pennine Way, and we might be tempted to rest a while and look around. The North Sea coast lies close at hand, and as we look at the distant lines of beaches and the wide horizon of the sea we shall be conscious that we have not only walked from Derbyshire to Scotland, but en route have crossed from the West Coast to the East.

Kirk Yetholm now lies straight below. There are no more hills to climb. It is going to be downhill all the way. Swinging round the shoulder of Black Hagg we make the steep descent of Halterburn. Legs feel like jelly at the speed of this descent but we are impelled to stride on in the thrilling climax of a journey. No obstacle lies in our way, no gulf to cross or crag to climb; only an easy winding track that takes us on to end our day in Yetholm.

This was the home of a notorious gipsy clan and the Gipsy Coronation was re-enacted in the summer of 1959 when Garnet Tice took the place of the King. The last real crowning took place in 1898, when Charles Faa Blyth took the throne, and the lineage can be traced back through the centuries to Anthony Gavin in 1506. A line of cottages across from the thatched *Border Hotel* is still called Gipsy Row, and a small cottage with an ivy-fronted porch retains its name as the Gipsy Palace. The main street of one-storied houses leads to a 16th century church with nimble little pinnacles at the corners of its towers. In the churchyard lies the tombstone of the last of the gipsy clan.

Hotels, a campsite and a delightful Youth Hostel established in an old school building are all to hand, you lay down your rucksack and suddenly feel so light of foot that you seem to glide across the ground. Thus we reach Kirk Yetholm, home of the gipsies and the end of the Pennine Way. But stay awhile before you enter by this track. Pause at the gate—and look back.

There lie the Cheviots crowned purple and gold, and not only the Cheviots, but the whole of the Pennines laid out below. And all this is yours for you have walked over it, and now it is part of you. Nothing will ever take it away, for this is your heritage.

This is the Pennine Way.

Planning an Expedition
along the Pennine Way

One of the problems of a long trek is the maintenance of dry and clean clothing. This can be overcome by arranging in advance for parcels to be forwarded to strategic points (complete with spare string and reversible outer wrapping paper for the return of soiled clothing) or else to be completely self-contained and ensure that in the evening you have a dry change within the rucksack. Plastic bags are a great asset in this respect, ensuring a dry compartment regardless of weather. A small packet of soap powder is worth carrying to enable the washing of clothes to take place en route. Those staying overnight in hostels or other accommodation have no difficulties in this respect, but campers might well choose a warm, sunny day (with luck!) to settle down by a stream or river and have a long break for washing and for cooking a mid-day meal. In this way, the heat of the day is avoided for strenuous trekking, the party is refreshed by the meal and linen has been washed and dried. Drip dry clothing is an asset here.

Light clothing is always an advantage on a strenuous trail such as the Pennine Way and during most of the year, shorts much preferable to long trousers. The latter should always be carried of course for the weather can be savage at times, but in wet weather or in striding across moorland and wild country, there is no comparison in the respective comfort. I know countless cases where those in long trousers have slipped into bog and continued the remainder of the route with the unpleasant reminder every time it rains or they walk through wet vegetation. Legs are easily washed and are dry almost as soon as the rain stops or you pass from wet grasses to shallow turf.

My groups invariably wear shorts and open neck shirts with thin and thick pullovers (worn as required, singly or paired) and the outer layer of windproof anorak and/or cagoule. Vests are deemed unsatisfactory since they retain moisture and tend to increase sweating discomforts. Light clothing which is loose fitting allows adequate ventilation and prevents uncomfortable overheating with the consequent slower pace. If it becomes wet during inclement weather, it dries almost as soon as the weather clears and with a minimum of discomfort. Trekking along the Pennine Way is warm work and the extra pullovers and windproof(s) will be more than adequate for any but wild winter conditions.

From early September to late April, full winter kit including headgear and gloves should be carried although not necessarily worn. Having it ready at the top of the pack is a convenient answer to this problem where safety factors must prevail. Boots and thick socks are not only the most comfortable footwear, they are also the safest. Should any foot discomfort arise, stop immediately and apply a dressing of zinc tape to the affected part. Prompt action will prevent a blister forming. Frequent bathing of the feet helps to keep them in good trim but if blisters do form, renew the plasters two or three times a day and if necessary protect further with antiseptic ointment (acriflex) which acts also as a lubricant. They may not heal in this arduous trail, but by these means you may rest assured that they will remain free from infection and will not give discomfort. A hole cut into a corn plaster pad is a very effective way of treating a blister, allowing it to heal without further pain during continued trekking.

Campers may not be able to dry out wet clothing during the evening, but they should not make the mistake of wearing the spare dry clothing on the following day. If further rain is encountered, both sets would be wet, and there would be no dry change for the night. The spare set should be stowed safely in its plastic bag, deep within the rucksack and the wet clothing put on to start the day. If the day is dry, the clothing quickly corresponds; on a wet day, nothing is lost! But at least, a dry change is assured when the camp is established in the evening.

Mountain safety depends equally on adequate feeding, and failure to maintain body reserves is a sure way to invite exhaustion, a slower pace, and the risk of exposure. It serves little to offer the prospect of a big meal later in the day unless the expended energy is constantly fed by new reserves. Accordingly, it is well to stop every two hours for a concentrated snack. The old safeguard for mountaineers — "eat a little very often" is very sound advice. My groups required feeding every hour on the final stretch!

As in any expedition, the task resolves into selecting the points where the proposed route might afford an overnight stay, allow for food provisions and maintain suitable distances which might generally be traversed within the daylight hours. To some extent the terrain will dictate its own terms: in the old days it was necessary to carry provisions for the completely savage thirty-seven miles from Edale to Hebden Bridge, but this has been cut by the provision of the Park Hostel at Crowden (15 miles) where both food and accommodation are provided for members and non-members alike. A further Youth Hostel is also available along the diversionary route at Marsden, although this does not provide more than sleeping and cooking facilities and food will have to be bought. Early closing days or week-ends might offer problems in planning food supplies if not envisaged. R.A.C. and A.A. guides often give early closing as well as suitable addresses for accommodation if you have no personal contact with the area. The final forty-three miles from Bellingham to Kirk Yetholm might well require that you carry 3 days' provisions unless you are sure that the store at Byrness is open.

To traverse the Pennine Way in sixteen days requires a daily average of over fifteen miles, probably with a full pack. However, the uneven nature of the terrain and the position of supply points entail a succession of "heavy" days with over twenty miles of rough going, followed by "light" days of perhaps only twelve (over easier ground).

An essential to any journey is to maintain the body reserves by eating well. Accordingly, a snack should be eaten about every two hours in addition to a full cooked breakfast and evening dinner.

The following Ordnance Survey 1:50 000 Sheets cover the Pennine Way:-110 (Edale - Standedge); 109 (Standedge - Warland Reservoir approach); 103 (Warland Reservoir - Airton); 98 (Kirkby Malham - Kisdon); 91 (Keld - Pikeman Hill); 86 (Garrigill - North Tyne approach); 80 (North Tyne - Auchope Cairn); 74 (The Cheviot - Kirk Yetholm). In addition, Sheets 104 and 92 will respectively be required for diversions to Haworth and Bowes.

The following 1:25 000 Outdoor Leisure Maps clearly mark the route of The Pennine Way:

The Dark Peak — Kinder, Bleaklow to Black Hill.

South Pennines — M62 crossing to Ponden (East of Colne).

Malham and Upper Wharfedale — Gargrave to Horton in Ribblesdale.

The Three Peaks — Fountains Fell to Hawes and Great Shunner Fell.

The above sequence of maps is in order of usage from south to north. Current editions mark the footpath "Pennine Way", but in the old one-inch series the footpath was rarely distinguished from any others and it was necessary to check the stages of the route with the Ramblers' Association pamphlet of the same name and obtainable from their headquarters at 1/4 Crawford Mews, York Street, London W1H 1PT (12p).

Itinerary for the Traverse

Start (Southern)

New O.S. 1:50000 Sheet 110 Sheffield and Huddersfield (or old one-inch O.S. Sheet 102).

Walking speeds are based on the assumption that a pack is carried.

Youth Hostel (Superior Grade), Rowland Cote, Nether Booth, Edale, Sheffield S30 2ZH. G.R. 139865. Store at Hostel. No closing day. Tel.: (0433) 70225. Next Hostel—Crowden—15 miles.

Edale Post Office and store, 2 miles. (Early closing Wednesday.)

Information Centre and campsite: The Warden, Fieldhead Campsite, Edale, Sheffield, S30 2ZA. Tel.: (0433) 70216.

Church Hotel, Edale, Sheffield—Tel.: (0433) 702681.

Please Note: Where closing days are given for hostels, these might not apply during the summer months when the majority remain open. Full details from Y.H.A., Trevelyan House, St. Albans, Herts.

Stage 1

New 1:50000 Sheet 110 (old one-inch Sheet 102), or special 1:25000 Tourist Map, "The Dark Peak".

Trek over Kinder Scout and Bleaklow to Crowden National Park Hostel (Standard Grade)—15 miles, or to Standedge (23 miles, severe country). Estimated walking speed throughout—2 m.p.h. (Backpacking).

Peak National Park Hostel, Crowden, Hadfield, Hyde, Cheshire SK14 7HZ. G.R. 073993. Tel.: Glossop (04574) 2135. Small store at hostel. Standard Grade. Closed Monday. Offers the first point for provisions, meals or accommodation. Dormitory or private single/double rooms for both Y.H.A. members or non-members. Next hostels: Marsden (14 miles) or Mankinholes Hall (27 miles). Standedge—possible moorland camp (23 miles from start).

Stage 2

New 1:50000 Sheets 110 and 103 (old one-inch Sheets: 102, 101 and 95). To Stoodley Pike or Hebden Bridge (14 miles). **Total:** 37 miles. Walking speed 2 m.p.h. throughout.

Supplies: A58 (White House Inn). Tel.: Littleborough 78456 (minor supplies or accommodation).

Accommodation: W. Jones, New Inn, Manchester Road, Marsden—Tel.: (0484) 844384. Marsden Youth Hostel (Simple Grade), The old Co-op, 1 Binn Road, Marsden, Huddersfield, West Yorkshire, HD7 6HF. G.R. 048112. Closed Thursday. Tel.: Huddersfield (0484) 843053. Small store at hostel. Shop and P.O. nearby. Early closing Marsden, Tuesday and Saturday. Mrs. H. Jackson, Old Edge, Colden, Hebden Bridge. Tel.: (9684) 4194. G.R. 956293. Mrs. J. Sunderland, High Greenwood House, Heptonstall, Hebden Bridge. Tel.: (9684) 2287. G.R. 963297.

Next hostel—Mankinholes Hall (17 miles by Pennine Way). Simple grade. Closed Wednesday. Mankinholes Hall, Todmorden, Lancashire, OL14 6HR. G.R. 960235. Tel.: Todmorden 070681. Store at hostel. Shops, hotels and P.Os in Todmorden and Hebden Bridge. Early closing: Tuesday.

Next Hostel: Haworth—15 miles (requires new O.S. 1:50000 Sheet 104 (old one-inch Sheet 96). Alternative: Earby—25 miles.

Stage 3

Stoodley Pike to Lothersdale. New 1:50000 Sheet 103 (old one-inch O.S. Sheet 95). Walking speed—2 m.p.h. to Heptonstall Moor; 3 m.p.h. thereafter. 17 miles. **Total:** 54 miles.

Accommodation: Sutcliffes, Colden Row, Heptonstall (Tel.: 2479); Ponden Hall, Stanbury, Keighley BD22 0HR (West Yorks.). Tel.: Haworth 44154.

Youth Hostel (Superior Grade) at Haworth—Longlands Hall, Lees Lane, Haworth, Keighley, West Yorkshire, BD22 8RJ. (New 1:50000 Sheet 104; one-inch O.S. Map Sheet 96). G.R. 038378. Tel.: Haworth 42234. Store at hostel. Closed Sunday. Shops, accommodation and P.O. in village (early closing Wednesday). Although slightly off the direct route of the Pennine Way, Haworth, with all its associations with the Brontës and the thriving Worth Valley Railway of the steam era, more than repays those prepared to stretch their legs for the few extra miles. Next hostel: Earby (15 miles via the Pennine Way).

Local store at Cowling (early closing—Saturday).

Recommended accommodation and campsite: Mr. and Mrs. Burnop, Woodhead Farm, Lothersdale, Keighley, Yorkshire. Tel.: Crosshills 32540.

Stage 4

Lothersdale to Malham. New 1:50000 Sheets 103 and 98 (old one-inch O.S. Sheets 95 and 90). 16 miles. **Total:** 70 miles.

Relatively easy ground—walking speed 3 m.p.h.

Earby Youth Hostel—The Katharine Bruce Glasier Memorial Hostel, Glen Cottage, Birch Hall Lane, Earby, Colne, Lancashire, BB8 6JX. Standard Grade. Closed Monday. G.R. 915468. Tel.: (0282) 842349. Small store at hostel. No meals provided. Shops and P.O. in village (early closing—Saturday). Next Hostel: Malham—15 miles.

Post Office and store at Thornton-in-Craven (59 miles). Early closing—Wednesday.

Gargrave (64 miles)—many shops with ample supply of provisions. Early closing: Tuesday. Singing Kettle Cafe, 60 High Street, Gargrave, Skipton, North Yorkshire—open 10 a.m. to 6 p.m. including Sundays; closed Monday; Tel.: Gargrave 252. Accommodation: Kirk Syke Private Hotel, High Street, Gargrave, Tel.: Gargrave 356.

Malham—Post Office, cafes, hotels, general stores, campsites and Youth Hostel. Early closing in village—Friday. Campsite: Mr. Moon, Townhead Farm, Malham, Skipton, North Yorkshire, Tel.: Airton 310. Youth Hostel (Superior Grade): The John Dower Memorial Hostel, Malham, Skipton, North Yorkshire, BD23 4DE. G.R. 901629. Tel.: Airton (07293) 321. Store at Hostel. Next Hostel, Stainforth—8 miles or Hawes—28 miles (very strenuous).

Other accommodation in Malham: Beck Hall (Mr. Boatwright), Malham, for those who enjoy old world furnishings, antiques and four poster beds! Parties catered for—Tel.: Airton 332. Buck Inn, Malham, Skipton, N. Yorks., Tel.: Airton 317. Sparth House, Malham, Skipton, Tel.: Airton 315 (special winter terms).

Stage 5

Malham to Horton-in-Ribblesdale (two summits). New 1:50000 O.S. Sheet 98 (old one-inch O.S. Sheet 90). Walking speed 2 m.p.h. 15 miles. **Total:** 85 miles.

Accommodation: Crown Hotel, Horton-in-Ribblesdale, Settle, North Yorkshire, Tel.: Horton-in-Ribblesdale (07296) 209. Mrs. C. Wilcock, Harber Farm, Horton-in-Ribblesdale, Tel.: (07296) 265.

Supplies: Penyghent Cafe, Horton-in-Ribblesdale. Tel.: (07296) 333. Peter and Joyce Bayes have a special welcome for Pennine Way parties—massive pots of tea, expedition foods, Pennine Way motifs and a unique log book for Pennine Way travellers to record their passage. Many write to confirm completion of the trek and the accounts of exploits make an interesting record of events. Pennine Way books, maps and outdoor equipment available. Open daily 9 a.m. to 6 p.m.

Nearest Youth Hostel—Stainforth (Standard Grade—closed

Thursday). Stainforth Hostel, Stainforth, Settle, North Yorkshire, BD24 9PA. G.R. 821668. Tel.: Settle (07292) 3577. Store in hostel. Shop and P.O. in village (early closing Wednesday). Next Hostel—Hawes (23 miles by the Pennine Way).

Campsite—Mr. Maudsley, Stainforth Hall Farm, Stainforth, Settle, North Yorkshire. Tel.: Settle (07292) 2200. This is an excellent campsite with access to the superb swimming pools below Stainforth Foss. Stainforth lies some 3½ miles south of the Pennine Way at Horton.

Stage 6

Horton-in-Ribblesdale to Hawes. Easy 13 miles. **Total:** 98 miles. New O.S. 1:50000 Sheet 98 (old one-inch O.S. Sheet 90). Walking speed 3 m.p.h.

Youth Hostel (Superior Grade): Hawes Youth Hostel, Lancaster Terrace, Hawes, North Yorkshire, DL8 3LQ. G.R. 867897. Tel.: Hawes (09697) 368. Store at Hostel (closed Monday). Shops and P.O. in village. Early closing day—Wednesday:; Market day—Tuesday. Next Hostel: Keld—9 miles.

Other accommodation: Mrs. Carr, Laburnum House, Hawes, Tel.: 380. Many other hotels and guest houses available. Miss Shay, The Green Dragon Inn, Hardraw, Hawes, Tel. Hawes 392.

Campsite: Mr. Dinsdale, Brown Moor Farm, Hawes, North Yorkshire (adjacent to river bridge). Tel.: Hawes (09697) 338. Full facilities.

Stage 7

Hawes to Keld. Walking speed 2½ m.p.h. 12 miles. **Total:** 110 miles. New O.S. 1:50000 Sheets 98 and 91 (old one-inch Sheet 90).

Accommodation and meals: Thwaite—Mrs. S. Hunter, Kearton Guest House, Thwaite, Tel.: Gunnerside (074886) 277. Keld: Mrs. Anderson, Rose Cottage, Keld. Miss Calvert, Woodside, Thorns, Keld, Tel.: (074886) 304. Mr. Rukin, Park Lodge Farm, Keld (both accommodation and campsite), Tel.: (074886) 274.

Keld Youth Hostel: Keld Lodge, Keld, Richmond, N. Yorkshire, DL11 6LL. Standard Grade. Closed Tuesday. G.R. 892009. Store at Hostel. Tel.: Gunnerside (074886) 259. P.O. nearby (early closing—Tuesday). Next Hostel—Barnard Castle (footpath 15 miles).

Stage 8

Keld to God's Bridge (Pasture End) or Bowes. Walking speed 3 m.p.h. 10 or 12 miles. **Total:** 120 or 122 miles. New O.S. 1:50000 Sheet 91 and 92 (old one-inch O.S. Sheets 90 and 84).

Campsite: J. Rowlandson, West Pasture End, Bowes.

Bowes: Many shops for provisions. Meals and accommodation to hand. Dotheboys Hall (Dickens). Mrs. Walker, The Grove Guest House, Bowes, Barnard Castle, Co. Durham, Tel.: Bowes 217.

Barnard Castle Youth Hostel, 91 Galgate, Barnard Castle, Co. Durham, DL12 8ES. Standard Grade. Store at Hostel, G.R. 053168. Tel.: Barnard Castle (08333) 2127. Closed Sunday. Many shops, hotels and P.O. nearby. (Early closing day, Thursday). Next Hostel: Langdon Beck—17 miles.

Stage 9

Alternative routes from God's Bridge (Pasture End) **or** from Bowes to Langdon Beck. Pasture End to Langdon Beck: 17 miles (**Total:** 137 miles). Bowes to Langdon Beck: 19 miles (**Total:** 141 miles). Strenuous day. Walking speed 3 m.p.h. to High Force reduced to 2 m.p.h. along the Tees thereafter. N.B. The diversion to Bowes entails a total addition of four miles. New O.S. 1:50000 Sheets 91 and 92 (old one-inch O.S. Sheet 84).

Supplies and accommodation at Middleton-in-Teesdale. Early closing day, Wednesday: Mrs. R. Bottomley, Blue Bell House, Market Place, Middleton-in-Teesdale, Co. Durham, Tel.: M.-in-T. 584. Mrs. A. Peacock, Green Gates, Middleton-in-Teesdale, Tel.: M.-in-T. 447.

Langdon Beck: High Force Hotel, Forest in Teesdale, Barnard Castle, Co. Durham. Tel.: Forest in Teesdale (083322) 264.

Youth Hostel, Langdon Beck, Forest in Teesdale, Barnard Castle, Co. Durham, DL12 0XN. G.R. 860304. Standard Grade. Closed Tuesday. Tel.: Forest in Teesdale (083322) 228. Store at Hostel. Next Hostel: Dufton—12 miles.

Camping at Hill End Farm, Forest in Teesdale—or an additional three miles will bring you to what was formerly one of the most remote spots in the Pennines, Caldron Snout (before the building of Cow Green Dam).

Stage 10

Langdon Beck to Dufton. Moderate day: walking speed 2½ m.p.h. 15 miles. **Total:** 152 miles. New O.S. 1:50000 Sheets 92 and 91 (old one-inch O.S. Sheets 84 and 83).

Accommodation: Mrs M.M. Lightburn, Norfolk House, Dufton, Appleby, Cumbria. Tel.: (0930) 51002.

Camping: David Howe, Dufton Hall Farm, Dufton, Appleby.

Supplies: The Post Office, Dufton, Appleby (early closing Saturday, but open on Sunday morning).

Youth Hostel, "Redstones", Dufton, Appleby, Cumbria, CA16 6DB. G.R. 688251. Tel.: Appleby (0930) 51236. Standard

Grade. Store at Hostel. Closed Monday. Next Hostel: Alston
—22 miles.

Stage 11

Dufton to Alston. Strenuous day. Walking speed 2 m.p.h. 22
miles. **Total:** 174 miles. New O.S. 1:50000 Sheets 91, 86 and
87 (old one-inch O.S. Sheets 83 and 84).

Accommodation and supplies: H. Jameson, Bleagate Farm,
Garrigill. Mrs. Bramwell, The Post Office, Garrigill—Tel.:
257. Early closing Tuesday.

Alston: Many guest houses, hotels and shops for provisions.
(Early closing day—Tuesday). Cumberland Hotel, Town
Foot, Alston, Cumbria (Tel.: Alston 245). Mrs. M. Ritchie,
Cragside Guest House (Tel.: Alston 420). Campsite between
the station and the South Tyne (H. Varty, Willows site).

Youth Hostel, The Firs, Alston, Cumbria (Superior Grade).
G.R. 717461. Tel.: Alston 509. Small store at Hostel. Closed
Thursday. Next Hostels: Greenhead (17 miles by Pennine
Way) or Once Brewed—24 miles.

Stage 12

Alston to Once Brewed Hostel. Easy start along the South
Tyne becoming more strenuous after Greenhead. Walking
speed 3 m.p.h. for first 15 miles (Greenhead) and 2 m.p.h.
for the remaining seven miles along the Wall to Once
Brewed Hostel. 22 miles. **Total:** 196 miles. New O.S. 1:50000
Sheet 86 (old one-inch O.S. Sheets 83, 76 and 77).

Burnstones Farm, one mile north of Slaggyford—excellent
meals and accommodation. Camping: Mr. Bowden, Wydon
Eals, Featherstone Park, South Tyne. Greenhead Youth
Hostel, Greenhead, Carlisle, Cumbria CA6 7HG. Tel.:
Gilsland (06972) 401. G.R. 659655. Closed Tuesday. Store at
Hostel. Early closing in village (shop and P.O.), Wednesday.
Next Hostel: Once Brewed—7 miles. Campsite: Calvoran
Farm, Greenhead, Carlisle, Cumbria.

Accommodation: Mrs. Bell, Fourwynds, Longbyre, Greenhead
—Tel.: Gilsland 330; Twice Brewed Inn, Military Road,
Bardon Mill, Northumberland, NE47 7AN—Tel.: Bardon
Mill 228; Mrs. Lawson, Winshields, Military Road, Bardon
Mill, Hexham—Tel.: Bardon Mill 243; Vallum Guest House,
Military Road, Bardon Mill, Hexham, Northumberland,
NE47 7AN—Tel.: Bardon Mill 248.

Once Brewed Youth Hostel, Military Road, Bardon Mill, Hex-
ham, Northumberland, NE47 7AN. Superior Grade. Tel.:
Bardon Mill (04984) 360. G.R. 752668. Store at Hostel.
P.O. Bardon Mill—3 miles (early closing—Thursday).
Information Centre alongside Hostel. Next Hostel:
Bellingham 18 miles (14 by footpath).

Stage 13

Once Brewed to Bellingham. Walking speed 2½ m.p.h. 14 miles. **Total:** 210 miles. New O.S. 1:50000 Sheets 86 and 80 (old one-inch O.S. Sheet 77).

Bellingham. Many shops for provisions (early closing—Thursday). Accommodation: Mrs. M. Thompson, 2 Fountain Terrace, Bellingham, Hexham, Northumberland—Tel.: Bellingham (0660) 321; Mr. Piercy Dixon, The Cheviot, Bellingham —Tel. (0660) 216; J. Brownbridge, Rose and Crown—Tel. (0660) 202; Mrs. Charles, The Rectory, Bellingham—Tel. (0660) 20225.

Youth Hostel, Woodburn Road, Bellingham, Hexham, Northumberland, NE48 2ED. G.R. 843834. Tel.: Bellingham (0660) 20313. Simple Grade. No store. No meals provided. Non VAT. Next Hostel: Byrness—15 miles.

Campsite at Bellingham: J. Wright, The Eals, Bellingham.

Stage 14

Bellingham to Byrness. Walking speed 2½ m.p.h. 15 miles. **Total:** 225 miles. New O.S. 1:50000. Sheet 80 (old one-inch O.S. Sheet 70).

Accommodation: Mrs A. Elliott, Spithopehead Farm, Byrness, Newcastle-upon-Tyne; Byrness Hotel—Tel.: Otterburn (0830) 20231. Shop, provisions etc., at nearby campsite.

Byrness Youth Hostel, 7 Otterburn Green, Byrness, Newcastle-upon-Tyne, NE19 1TS. Standard Grade. Non VAT. G.R. 764027. Tel.: Otterburn (0830) 20222. Small store at Hostel. Shop and P.O. nearby—early closing day Saturday. Next Hostel: Kirk Yetholm (SYHA)—27 miles by path. Campsites—better on higher ground when midges prevail.

Stages 15 and 16

From Byrness across the Cheviots to Kirk Yetholm. Very strenuous country. 27 miles (including two mile return ascent of Cheviot). Walking speed 2 m.p.h. **Total:** 252 miles. New O:S. 1:50000 Sheet 80 (old one-inch O.S. Sheets 70 and 71).

The final crossing of the Cheviots will have to be completed in one day by those who do not camp. However, their packs will tend to be lighter than those carried by campers and in their case an average walking speed of 2½ m.p.h. would be a fair estimate for the full crossing. All walking speeds have been estimated for persons carrying camping equipment and persons carrying only minor loads will travel a half to a full mile an hour faster,

On this final stage, the weather conditions will determine where the campers will spend the night; the first stage involving the heavy climb might be the shorter distance to the exposed campsite at

1,800 ft., Windy Rigg (12 miles). The more sheltered site at Chew Green might even be reached on the previous day from Bellingham to make a total of 19 miles for that day. Otherwise, there are many sheltered sites below the summits (lee side) or the less attractive alternative of an enforced descent to lower ground. Do not think that once you have reached the main height it will be easy. The tufted vegetation will slow your progress.

Accommodation at Kirk Yetholm:

The Youth Hostel, Kirk Yetholm, Kelso, Roxburghshire. G.R. 826282. No store or meals provided in this simple hostel (SYHA). Normally open Easter to October only. (Warden lives in house next to Border Hotel).

Shops in Kirk Yetholm (early closing—Saturday) or in Town Yetholm (1 mile) where the early closing is Wednesday.

Several Hotels: Plough Hotel, Town Yetholm (Tel. Yetholm 215), White Swan Hotel, Town Yetholm, Kelso (Tel. Yetholm 249).

Campsite: Mrs. Gibsom, The Garage, Town Yetholm or Mr. Robb, Blunty's Mill, Kirk Yetholm (Tel. Yetholm 288).

Mountain Rescue Unit based at Yetholm may be alerted from the police station (Yetholm 217).

Two wooden refuges on the Cheviots:

G.R. 805129 Yearning Saddle—wooden refuge hut built in 1967: ½ mile S.W. of Lamb Hill by Border Fence.

G.R. 875202 Red Cribs—between the Schil and Auchope Cairn by the Border Fence, an old goods waggon (field telephone for emergencies).

I am indebted to my colleagues Roger Markendale and Chris Hart for these latter observations during recent traverses.

Towns which are not within easy walking distance of the Pennine Way have not been mentioned, but where a party has supporting transport there is no difficulty in obtaining provisions from such places. The use of A.A. or R.A.C. Guides is a simple way of determining early closing days and details of hotels, etc. The Ramblers' Association Bed, Breakfast and Bus Guide (published by the Ramblers' Association, 1/4 Crawford Mews, York Street, London W1H 1PT) gives very full details of places offering accommodation along the Pennine Way. Also from the same address, the Pennine Way route guide, 12p.

I have already stressed that good feeding is one of the essentials for safety on the hills, and for the long distance trekker the whole success of the venture may well depend upon catering arrangements. The following suggestions offer guidance in the preparation of packed lunches with varied items which may be eaten as snacks at two hourly intervals as required. Include at least one item from each grouping:

(1)   Protein—Hard boiled egg **or** 3oz Cheese **or** 3oz Corned Beef or similar tinned meat **or** 3 oz. polony, salami, etc. Meat pie.

(2)   Carbohydrate—4 oz. biscuits (8 oz. pkt. per two—vary daily). Freshly made sandwiches from teacakes, sliced bread, etc., with suitable fillings.

(3)   4 oz. dried fruit—3 oz. raisins and 1 oz. nuts; 4 oz. dates, apricots, etc. Fruit bars.

(4)   Fresh fruit or vitamin "C" tablets.

(5)   Boiled sweets, chocolate, Kendal Mint Cake, glucose, etc.

In addition to the above, a fully cooked breakfast and three course evening meal should be routine. Some care in the planning of the meals will ensure good morale within the party, and whether camping, hostelling or whatever, a good brew **on arrival** is a sure stimulus to the additional energy boost which may be required in the preparation of the substantial evening meal. Campers, in particular, will have to consider the total cooking time required as well as the restricted number of pans and burners available. This is essential when fuel may be restricted and everything has to be carried. Keeping the lid on the pan except for stirring saves fuel. Meat and hard vegetables which may require a full hour's cooking should be the first items on the stove, and after boiling for some ten minutes should be lifted off to a flat stone while the next pan (soup?) is brought to the boil. As long as the lid remains firmly fixed on the first pan, the cooking will continue on the stone for a little while and the pan should be returned to the stove periodically to bring back to full heat. By this means, several pans may be kept at simmering point and a full three course meal served piping hot from one stove.

The sixteen day schedule has been accomplished by many camping parties, but if time permits, it is worth an additional day to explore the Malham area and possibly to divide the Alston/Twice Brewed section in two days. If sixteen days is more than can be spared, one day can be saved by combining stages 6 and 7, Horton-in-Ribblesdale to Keld, and another by ensuring the crossing of the Cheviots in one day to cut the complete journey to fourteen days.

A Pennine Way Council, under the chairmanship of Tom Stephenson, has been formed to secure the protection of the Pennine Way, to provide information about the Way to the public and to assist the different interests connected with the Way. Members of the Council are basically Local Authorities adjoining the Way and representatives from interested voluntary societies. The Council publishes an "Accommodation List" of recommended bed and breakfast type places convenient for walkers of the Way, available from the Ramblers' Association Head Office, London.

A Bibliography

Geology and Scenery of England and Wales	A.E. Trueman	Pelican
Mountains and Moorlands ...	W.H. Pearsall	Collins
Flowers of Chalk and Limestone	J.E. Lousley	Collins
The Face of North-west Yorkshire	Raistrick & Illingworth	Dalesman
Longdendale	K. Oldham	—
Mountain Trail	J. Wood	Unwin
A guide to the Cheviot Hills	F.R. Banks	Reid
Journey into Roman Britain	G.M. Durant	Bell
The Pennines and Adjacent Areas (Geology)	D.A. Wray	H.M.S.O.
British Regional Geology Northern England	T. Eastwood	H.M.S.O.
Housesteads Roman Fort ...	E. Birley	H.M.S.O.
Around Ingleton and Clapham		Dalesman
Yorkshire's Three Peaks ...		Dalesman
Malham		Dalesman
Camping and Exploration ...	K. Oldham	—

The author acknowledges the help of many Pennine Way walkers who have kindly contributed recent information concerning places to stay. This is much appreciated as the work is continually being revised and it is a great asset to be able to pass on details of places where Pennine Way walkers are made most welcome.